encounter

The Theory and Practice
of Encounter Groups

encounter

ARTHUR BURTON, EDITOR

Jossey-Bass Inc., Publishers
615 Montgomery Street · San Francisco · 1970

ENCOUNTER
The Theory and Practice of Encounter Groups
Arthur Burton, Editor

Copyright © 1969 by Jossey-Bass, Inc., Publishers

Copyright under Pan American and
Universal Copyright Conventions

Jossey-Bass, Inc., Publishers
615 Montgomery Street
San Francisco, California 94111

Library of Congress Catalog Card Number 73-92889

Standard Book Number SBN 87589-044-X

Manufactured in the United States of America
Composed and printed by York Composition Company, Inc.
Bound by Chas. H. Bohn & Co., Inc., New York

JACKET DESIGN BY WILLI BAUM, SAN FRANCISCO

Code 6914

THE JOSSEY-BASS BEHAVIORAL SCIENCE SERIES

General Editors

WILLIAM E. HENRY
University of Chicago

NEVITT SANFORD
Stanford University and Wright Institute, Berkeley

PREFACE

Encounter groups have been so busy being expressive that they have had little time to look to their theories. But history demonstrates that a technique without a rationale eventually falls into disuse. And, interestingly enough, those in the vanguard of the encounter movement, the leaders and group facilitators themselves, have been notoriously unresponsive to the self-demand for theoretical clarification. There are, of course, several reasons for this. The first is perhaps the belief that intellectual constructions at this point in the development of encounter are inadvisable and defeat the purpose for which the movement was itself initially established. The second might be that it is too early for a theory of encounter—that psy-

choanalysis after more than a half-century of study is still without
a complete theory of human behavioral change. The third point is
that theories, in the final analysis, follow rather than precede action,
and encounter must first find ways of holding its dialogue before
it can theorize about what it does—or should do.

All of these suggested extrapolations for not theorizing seem
incorrect to me. The encounter movement has vast social ramifica-
tions and not merely for psychotherapy alone. I am in all serious-
ness when I say that it may soon represent the Judeo-Christian
emphasis on individualization applied to vast numbers of people
who can no longer be formally Christian but who want to be fully
human. The professionally religious have sensed this ahead of some
of the rest of us and this may explain their deep participation in
encounter work.

Some of the limitations of psychoanalysis, it seems to me,
were due to the fact that psychoanalytic insights came solely from
the crucible of the patient-analyst interaction, and Freud himself
had eventually to hide behind the couch to arrive at a proper intellectual perspective of his work. It is thus often important to re-
move oneself from the scene of battle and speculate about the
campaign itself. And only in this way can direction be given to the
next campaign.

This book attempts to fill the theoretical vacuum that now
exists in encounter work at the same time that it explicates a necessary methodology. Its contributors are precisely those scientists who
reflect deeply on what they do and are in addition not fearful of
the bold statement. Encounter now desperately requires a scientific
base and I hope this book will be one step in that necessary direction.

Davis, California   ARTHUR BURTON
September 1969

CONTENTS

CONTRIBUTORS

Arthur Burton, Ph.D., professor of psychology, Sacramento
State College

Meyer M. Cahn, Ph.D., professor of higher education, San
Francisco State College

Albert Ellis, Ph.D., executive director and supervisor of
clinical services, Institute for Advanced Study
in Rational Psychotherapy, New York

Bertram R. Forer, Ph.D., psychotherapist, Los Angeles

Jack R. Gibb, Ph.D., human relations consultant, La Jolla

Lorraine M. Gibb, M.A., human relations consultant, La Jolla

Thomas P. Malone, M.D., Ph.D., staff psychotherapist, Atlanta Psychiatric Clinic

Sumner B. Morris, Ed.D., director, Counseling Center, lecturer in psychology, University of California, Davis

Jack C. Pflugrath, Ph.D., counseling psychologist, University of California, Davis

Erving Polster, Ph.D., chairman, Post-Graduate Training Committee, Gestalt Institute, Cleveland

Stewart B. Shapiro, Ph.D., director of counseling and guidance, Graduate School of Education, University of California, Santa Barbara

Bernard Steinzor, Ph.D., psychotherapist, and lecturer, Program in Psychiatry and Religion, Union Theological Seminary, New York

Frederick H. Stoller, Ph.D., senior research associate and associate professor, University of Southern California

Barbara Taylor, M.A., counseling psychologist, University of California, Davis

Hobart F. Thomas, Ph.D., professor of psychology, Sonoma State College

John Warkentin, M.D., Ph.D., staff psychotherapist, Atlanta Psychiatric Clinic

encounter

The Theory and Practice of Encounter Groups

INTRODUCTION

Encounter:
An Overview

Arthur Burton

The significant thing about the chapters contained in this book is the conviction with which the writers speak. There is again an old-time fervor in psychic discovery earlier associated with psychoanalysis. This enthusiasm is not that of a brilliant new idea, or even of a creative technique that basically changes a human outlook of long standing. It is, rather, the impact of once again discovering the joy and growth that people can have in small, close peer relationships—and of personally experiencing it. That the psychoanalytic tradition needs revitalization goes without saying. But in this book there are no great insights to match those of the founders of psychoanalysis; there is only the ancient understanding that *community,* set in a framework of honesty, openness, and responsibility, is enlivening and healing. And this "community healing" is vastly different from group therapy or group recreation. Encounter groups are "soul" groups, in which the basic parameters of the human condition are opened for all persons to share. There is no agenda. What purpose there is is merely to live more fully and to experience more deeply. Personal history and conflict are temporarily set aside so that living itself may be experienced. In encounter living, it is then hoped, some of the answers to existence can be found.

Each author in this book testifies in his own way to this same discovery, and his chapter becomes a personal document as well as a scientific treatise. But I have insisted that each of us spells out—as best he can—what his operations in encounter groups are, and what are the theoretical constructs behind them. The fact that these demands are imperfectly met simply demonstrates that we are groping our way into uncharted fields. Carl Rogers has said that the encounter movement is the most significant social movement of our time. Is this too ambitious a statement? Possibly. But all of us who do encountering work believe that something unique, transporting, and unifying has been found which is unmatched thus far by classical psychotherapy. Encountering is intended not to replace psychotherapy, only to augment it.

Forer argues that growth and development are a process of becoming human. Modern life dissociates the individual and forces him to feel shame, guilt, and anxiety. He becomes ultimately fearful of his own expectations and settles for little. Encounter forces the client to experience himself totally, to verbalize his expectations, and to listen to his self-condemnations against the background of group response.

Steinzor sees an ossification in institutional approaches to healing and relates them to power struggles in society. He even labels community psychiatry a euphemism rather than a reality when applied to lower economic groups. Effective treatment must demonstrate care and concern on the part of the therapist and contact must involve increased emphasis on authenticity, congruence with one's feelings, and confrontation. This then serves to place one in the larger relationship of the community as a whole. Two-person and n + 2-person groups have the same values, but the latter give more facile opportunity for equity and intimacy to operate. But giving up the specific values of dyadic therapy comes with great difficulty for Steinzor.

The heart of encountering is reached by Thomas, who reports in a straightforward way his difficulties with self-realization under contemporary circumstances. He describes elementally the impact that meeting with another person in the group has upon him, and the relationship of one member to another. He describes self-goals against the background of group goals in the encounter group, and the resolution of both. Thomas' low-key, empathic, and sincere presentation is as convincing as his logic.

The goals of encounter groups for Stoller are "growth and change, new behavioral directions, the realization of potential, heightened self-awareness, and a richer perception of one's circumstances as well as the circumstances of others." While these are also obtainable through dyadic psychotherapy, the assumptions and procedures vary and a different image of man obtains in encountering. Problematic human beings maintain unused latencies, overinvest energy in one part of self, are unable to take risks, and their perception of their course in the world is dulled. Such conditions often create tensions and yearnings which are not necessarily neurotic. Group encounter helps dissipate such states by permitting people to rub up against one another and by revealing the reactions and reflections of the participants. The relationships and crises that develop in the encounter group are the fundamental laboratory for self-exploration and change. For Stoller, the marathon approach offers advantages that conventional encounter groups do not.

Cahn learns of his own self-deception in the group by writing poetry to a female member of his encounter group. While this seems to him at the time the height of feeling, the sober analysis that follows tells him that he has "copped out" in this unique way from knowing the person involved. His point is that artistry in any form

—poetry or whatever—may be supreme expression but is not the everyday grist of human interaction, and may, indeed, be a flight from it.

Ellis takes a critical stance toward traditional encounter groups. He would add the rational-emotive idea—the theoretical outlook he is particularly identified with—to the traditional encounter approach. He summarizes the principal arguments made against encounter groups and discusses their inadequacies as arguments. But he holds firmly that universal ideas of perfection, being loved by all, that people are wicked, that things have always to go right are a bill of goods. The rational-emotive group encounter approach helps to change such mythologies, which are found even in certain Esalen- and Synanon-type groups.

Malone wonders why some mornings he awakens and finds himself deeply aware of himself and totally expressive, and why, on other mornings, nothing works. He analyzes this phenomenon in relationship to his group encounter experiences and decides that one state involves logic and intellectualization and the other passion. Dyadic psychotherapy leans more toward the former and group encounter toward the latter. He makes the point that dyadic psychotherapy may make one unfit for a passionate group approach, or at least a relearning process of some moment may be required. Passion puts us in touch with the deepest feelings of the client, with the feelings about each other, and with their ecological ambiance.

Encounter groups are more closely related to the community at large than is traditional psychotherapy. Indeed, the encounter group is a microcommunity that mirrors and reflects the total community. Polster attempted an experiment of making a coffee shop audience a limited encounter group. He found the discussion related to race and other social problems rather than to intrapsychic obsession, and action rather than image the currency. He also found tremendously close personal involvement, release of aggressions without violence, and a greater sympathy for variegated social points of view in his experiment. Polster implies that encountering may be a useful approach to the resolution of social as well as personal problems.

Involvement and intensity are the key concepts for Warkentin. All that technique can do is to involve people, and group approaches are superior in this regard to individual ones. No emotional growth was possible for Robinson Crusoe until Friday came on the scene. Warkentin describes how he combines group with individual approaches regularly in his practice and some of the problems involved. He limns for us the role of the therapist in group encounter, and the many ways of stimulating intensity of feeling and relatedness. Fortunate strangers become significant others.

Shapiro offers the example of encounter work with church executives and points up their specific dehumanized existence. His specific contribution to the book is to delineate a method of approach called tradition innovation. This approach challenges accepted customs, rituals, and ways of behavior by improvising newer and more adequate ones within a climate of trust, which is the encounter group.

The Gibbs elaborate on their TORI (Trust-Openness-Realization-Interdependence) theory of organizational management and apply it to all human growth. Growth, which is common to all living organisms, is a movement from fear to trust, from restricted to open communication, from dependence to self-determination, from dependence to interdependence. TORI theory implies that the major barriers to growth are fears, distrusts, and invalid life theories. TORI provides the following correction: an experience of growing for each person; an experience of being a free member of a creative and growing group; an opportunity to try out new behaviors and feelings; an opportunity to develop new theories that integrate values and his world; and an opportunity to take full responsibility for behavior.

Encounter groups are being offered as the new educational methodology and several research centers are now empirically testing this approach. Morris and colleagues describe some of the ills of the contemporary learning process in higher education. They see today's students differing from those of a decade ago, more alert to the total meaning of life and to how education might help actualize it for them. They now ask such questions as, "What is the good life?"; "What is significant?"; "What is morality?"; "How can I love?"; "What is worthwhile?"; "What matters and what do

I stand for?"; "How can I make connections with my own feelings
and the feelings of others?" The encounter group approach, they
believe, explodes with antidotes to the dehumanization of education
by stressing openness, transparency, and clear and effective communication. What is real, actual, and here-and-now receives an
emphasis in encountering unmatched elsewhere. Self-learning becomes the core of all learning.

Burton, by way of further introduction, traces some of the
philosophic antecedents to the encounter group movement, its
needs, and some of its weaknesses. He sees encountering as a basic
variant of the healing process with a need for integration of dyadic
and polyadic processes. Most needed are a consistent and unified
theory of its operations and empirical assessment of its outcomes.

The total picture presented by the contributors to this
volume is one in which the responsibility for growth is actually returned to the person, one in which each of us is responsible as well
for the social action of our times. Encountering seems to be the
counterrevulsion to the denigration of the person in our times, and
the need to bring the person back into center focus. This is perhaps
why the encounter group is so popular with the new generation.

I

Encounter, Existence, and Psychotherapy

Arthur Burton

Encounter groups and group transactions are not merely abbreviated or less expensive ways of providing needed melioration but a significant alteration in the cultural norm by virtue of which society allows psychotherapy to persist at all. But has psychotherapy served its purpose? Is the sometimes violent attack upon its most sacred principles evidence that it is being systematically replaced? Do the variations themselves contain the phoenix for a new psychological approach to suffering, growth, and fulfillment? Is there a new cadre of practitioners in the wings quite unlike Freud himself? Before attempting to answer these general questions it might be helpful to consider several general background matters which set the tone for the discussion to follow.

Encounter groups[1] are now becoming so prevalent that they will soon constitute a secularized psychotherapy for Everyman.[2] By and large such groups are not led by psychoanalysts or psychiatrists but by people trained in the social and behavioral sciences.[3]

Group leaders also include in vast numbers teachers, ministers, publishers, artists, housewives, students, and a laity imbued with a certain call to rescue humanity. To identify the character of this new healing horde, it is indeed difficult to cling to the medical model; but it should be noted that the economics of medical psychotherapy have been carefully preserved in encounter work. And it represents for me psychological principles applied to healing and is therefore governed by all of the ethics of the healing encounter.

Encounter[4] is not an eleemosynary development and did not spring from the ghetto. It is intended not for the impoverished or the racially deprived but for the middle class, which still internalizes its problems and has historically been the best patron of psychotherapists. The group leaders themselves come from the same segment of society. In this sense the encounter reformation falls short of that sought-for universal or natural anodyne which, for example, the behavioral therapies attempt to provide.

But this is not the entire story. Psychotherapy is no longer

[1] I use this term to cover all sensitivity, awareness, meditative, body, consciousness-expanding, and other forms of current encounter experiences which take place in more than dyadic groups. Their diversities are often more apparent than real, so that lumping them here seems justified.

[2] A card has just reached my desk announcing that the January 26, 1969, television program of David Susskind would involve a discussion of marathon group encounters. Mr. Susskind is very shrewd in determining what the public wants and giving it to them.

[3] Professionals are even felt to offer less charisma or freedom to act than lay people who have found their own unique way to their being.

[4] The word *encounter* will be used throughout this paper not only to signify the encounter group movement in its varied manifestations, but also to mean the significant meeting of two people in a transcending matrix with the intention of growing through it. Dyadic encounter, while it is possibly encounter in some instances, will always be specified by the modifier *dyadic*.

for the diseased. Some form of it is demanded by large numbers of college students, management and supervisorial personnel, religious people, the formerly married, the unmarried, the sadly married, the literate, and the artistic and creatively inclined. It comes under many guises: fulfillment, realization, body-integration, awareness, sensory peaking, morale, efficiency, humanity, joy, peace, unity, love, nirvana, and others. Its tenets are being offered as a new method of general education—of emotional rather than cognitive learning. It is freedom's approach to growth—and the possibility of being in a world which now severely curtails existence. If the loss of the medical model comes it will not be on the basis of the arguments of Szasz,[5] but the fact that a medical technique reserved for the sick is now applied with beneficial effects to the well. I have in this regard elsewhere demonstrated that the concepts and techniques of healing are the same with the diseased as with the non-diseased.[6]

Those whom society labeled "average" or "normal" frequently resented their being placed in that existential limbo, resented the fact that their alienation, their loneliness, their despair, and their anxiety were ignored *because* they were normal. The normal have at times even produced symptoms to gain the center of the stage—the existential neuroses—but the entire question of the meaning of a flowering symptom is now a complex and confused one. A psychic symptom is today no longer a symptom but a sign that life lacks joy. The introduction of psychedelic drugs was a self-healing, a self-growth-inducing device that appeared when the institutional structure failed in some way to validate the young. It now seems certain to me that psychiatry as a discipline will ultimately devote itself exclusively to the psychotic, and this with improved biological weapons, while the question of personality growth will be left to the social scientists. And self-consciousness and the relationships between men have at any rate always been the latter's province, and social scientists were invariably better prepared to

[5] Szasz, T. *The Myth of Mental Illness.* New York: Harper, 1962.

[6] Burton, A. "The Psychotherapy of a Non-Diseased Person," in A. Burton (Ed.), *Modern Psychotherapeutic Practice.* Palo Alto: Science and Behavior Books, 1965.

deal with them once the medical stigmata were removed from the behavior involved. The creative imagination was indeed never the province of the physician, except perhaps in the time of Asclepius.

Rieff[7] is correct when he calls this age the Therapeutic Age. But what it is that is therapeutic in the Therapeutic Age has always been a confused and sometimes a sullen matter. Freud, within his biological goals the humanitarian, opted for just slightly reduced suffering for his hysterics, but he did not fool himself about the extraordinary effort it took to bring this about, and how rarely it occurred. But he really never held the lamp of being fully human very high. Freud basically took a dim view of the possibilities of self-realization and self-fulfillment, in the sense in which we understand them today. And not even an extraordinary Jew could divorce himself from the tragic sense of life which is the unconscious coloration of every historic Jewish person. Man he saw as always and everlastingly the predator.

The dismaying thing is that Freud's own inner joy—the pleasures of creative thought and writing—did not seem to influence his apperception of man as basically vicious. Despite his great artistry he mostly failed to see the curative, releasing, and growth-producing possibilities in the artistic production—except perhaps as a very minor sublimation. Jung was more fortunate in this regard because he was always more in touch with his personal muse. Maslow and his B-values would have been laughed out of the Vienna Circle because his approach could not genuinely be understood as relating to conflict and disease. The positive values of man thus got short shrift in early psychoanalysis—the reduction of the negative, the symptom, the pain, the disablement, became instead the major if not total focus.

Psychotherapists, as I have known them, have not seemed to me to be a particularly joyous group, and they seem rather to get their satisfactions in the same way Freud did—that is, by therapeutic cloistering with their clients, by the joyful manipulation of the symbolic monads of the psyche, by creative production, and

[7] Rieff, P. *The Triumph of the Therapeutic.* New York: Harper, 1966.

by a competitive friendship with their own kind. Their provincialism is in a way truly astonishing.

What has not always been so clearly understood is that psychoanalysis and psychoanalytic psychotherapy now represent the dominant morality of the age. Encounter becomes therefore a breaking with the morals of the fathers. It has always appeared to me that the psychotherapeutic situation is basically a Judeo-Christian "judgmental" one and no amount of beneficence and goodwill can change that elemental fact. A schizophrenic woman whom I labored mightily for years to help, and who *was* helped, wounded me at the end by saying that "after all, psychotherapy is an indignity." But after months of angry reflection, I now believe she may be correct in her statement.

Psychotherapy exhorts as it comforts, and it promises salvation in this life in the same way that theology promises it in the afterlife. The Jew has always been the archetypal sufferer in the cultural history of man. Making the best of it until the Messiah comes has been the consistent metaphysic of the Jew, and he still believes this, as the concentration camp experience has shown. The fact that so many Jews are impelled to become psychotherapists reveals the need to project their moral unconscious upon the world. The Jew does not proselyte or make converts to his religion. He does not have to. Psychoanalysis does it for him.

Freud himself was a highly moral man—perhaps overly moral for his own justified pleasures—and on a reactive formation basis it is easy to understand why he staked life and career on the Medusa of sex. Psychotherapists become upset with the off-beat client—the one who seriously departs from historical morality—and with the one who acts-out and fails to preserve the decorum of the analytic dance. This is really why so few chronic alcoholics, forgers, homosexuals, and criminals ever reach the analytic couch. It is simply not true that the psychotherapist regards all of his clients as unwashed lambs. The transference itself, and the analysis of the transference neurosis, is a dogmatized ritual by which a limited freedom-to-be is exchanged for a compromised moral peace with the Fathers.

Clients have always been dimly aware that psychoanalysis

and psychoanalytic psychotherapy were, so to speak, a bad social bargain, but they had no other recourse. This is why really so few psychotherapies ever reach the point that totally satisfies either the therapist or the client. The client invariably breaks the therapeutic contract when he has the strength to do so; but of course both parties rationalize his improvement—and he is often improved. The limits set on acting-out, loving-out, and living-out, the careful guarding of the therapist's own person, the rigid temporal parameters, the hush-hush conspiracy about money, the authoritarianism of the interpretation, the morality play, among others, have always been covertly resented by the client. In encounter, the client throws them all overboard. He can live, love, and act-out inside and outside of the encounter group,[8] has a passionate leader[9] instead of a moral therapist, time is rarely of the essence, and he can easily accept or reject any interpretation the group leader or any group member cares to make. The encounter group thus offers freedom from the modern repressive morality of the transference, but with the necessary retention of the releasing values of creative-formative insight and the sharpening of images, feelings, and archetypes long since placed in Pandora's limbo.

Most of the activist problems of today's society are, in my opinion, generation-gap problems, and psychology and psychiatry have no immunity from them. The generation gap is furthermore entirely a moral problem (in the widest sense); codified and solidified ways of thinking, feeling, and behaving, rather than age differences per se, are the sources of contention.[10] More than we realize, psychotherapy is an important social bulwark of conservative "holding the line," and it often has vested interests to equal any

[8] Many clients tell me that they go to encounter group centers not only for the encounter itself but for the vast opportunities for sexual experience which are to be found there. One famous encounter center offers baths in which mixed nude bathing is the rule after the sessions themselves. One invariably gets a chance there to live sexuality rather than learning how to displace or sublimate it.

[9] Thomas Malone's use of the word *passionate* to describe encounter seems to me a salubrious one.

[10] It is significant that the Haight-Ashbury hippy subculture, for example, accepted membership from persons of any age providing only the candidate met the requirements of dropout.

corporate power. Aggression, passivity, and nihilism are proper subjects for analysis but may not be used to overturn the system itself.[11] Encounter, however, changes the moral basis of treatment for it is a form of cultural revolution.

Just so long as culture extorts internalizing and symbolizing impulse, then the psychoanalytic process of slow and controlled externalization is a proper approach to growth. But unfortunately children no longer internalize and introject exactly the way Freud thought they did, and the hysteric is a vanishing breed in our time. Repression on the basis of infantile eroticism is much rarer today; so is the guilt that accompanied it. The child is less schizoid and forced to become a joiner and social participant whether he likes it or not and, if he later manifests an adult emotional problem, it is more apt to be a character warp than a matter of conversion. Children are now much more accepted as sexual beings, and may not only marry a few years after puberty, but are sexually experienced beyond their parents long before this. It is not always recognized that the personality problems connected with externalization can be as great as those which are related to internalization. But our therapeutics are sadly inward-looking and we mostly ignore, say, the arsonist. I have in this connection earlier referred to the gentle passivity of Freud himself as a style of life.

Encounter involves more a molar than molecular behavior— the act rather than the wish, or the external rather than the internal. It is possible in encounter to act despite one's repressions; and it is often possible immediately to release repression in one or more bursts of affection or aggression without the expected damage. I might aphoristically say that in encounter work the symbol is

[11] In observing the stresses and strains of the University of California and California State College System student, faculty, and administrative disaffections (January, 1969), as well as the neighboring black-white urban problems, I am struck at how rarely psychoanalytic intervention is called upon. The paradox is that psychoanalysts probably understand more about human aggression than any other single group in society, yet are rarely called upon to help resolve the social issues of our time. I believe this disablement stems from their special position as healers in society and the roles which evolve from it. Szasz surely exaggerates the police function of psychotherapy, but his thesis has considerable merit in that social "enforcers" rarely make social "policy" or even critical social decisions.

diminished for the transaction. In psychotherapy the symbol—the carrier of the forbidden wish—is of course king; in encounter the symbol is manifestly secondary.[12] Dream interpretation, the fundament of all psychotherapeutic technique, becomes therefore ancillary or even useless.

The body has been strangely missing in psychotherapy and encounter attempts to return it to man. Lowen,[13] while not necessarily an exponent of encountering, makes the most eloquent case for the unification of body and mind. It is paradoxical that the physician, who must have a fundamental training in biology, departs from the body when he becomes a psychiatrist, or at least is at a loss which to treat first when he gets his first patient. Encounter, on the other hand, gives the body primacy, and most encountering methods, possibly influenced by yoga, find a central position for bodily sensation and feeling.[14] The pristine joy of a unified body, without Christian sin, is a rare experience and one which fulfillment must countenance. The failure of orgasm has come to stand for the missing body and has itself become a fetish.

Increased conscious, sensory, and body awareness, as a form of encounter, is thus designed to return the body to the disembodied psyche, and to make it feel itself more acutely. There is no reason why a bowel movement, or a deferred urination, should not make its contribution to the hegemony of an individual, as it most certainly does in constipation or prostatitis.

More generically, psychotherapy quietly sets arbitrary epistemological limits by saying to the person, "it is dangerous for you to know this," or "it is dangerous for you to know it at this time." The fact that neuroses are by definition infantile drags on the

---

[12] I have attempted from time to time to offer interpretations to my encounter groups and found them uniformly rejected by the participants. This produced a great feeling of uselessness in me. This does not mean that interpretation has no place in encounter, but it does have very little place. Encounter is experientially introjective rather than interpretative and it places little premium on intelligence with its function of rapidly manipulating symbols and placing and displacing them.

[13] Lowen, A. *The Betrayal of the Body.* New York: Macmillan, 1967.

[14] See, for example, Gunther, B. *Sensitivity Awakening: Relaxation* (Long-play phonograph record). Big Sur, Calif.: Esalen Foundation, 1968.

personality does not necessarily require an infantile re-experiencing for their cure; logically, a case could indeed be made for a wider experiencing. Free association is not so free. The client ultimately supplies what he thinks the therapist wants. The psychotherapeutic imprimatur calls for a specific design of treatment, a coordinated timetable, in which, if the treatment falls off course, the therapist becomes irritable. The psychotherapist's personal or training analysis is his unconscious radar, by which he handles himself in critical moments—and he really never gets over that sacred event. In regressions in therapy he reverts again and again to it. This creates a curiously rigid structure within the process of freedom-to-be. Encounter opposes such unconscious rigidities as hypocrisy and seeks rather to "come on straight." Although it usually does, it has other serious problems.

Psychotherapy is conceptually composed of a few fundamental principles, which, while difficult of application, are easily seized upon by the laity for their specific purposes. Synanon, for example, encourages a hostile confrontation between members in what it calls "games," and it offers immediate catharsis of aggressive feeling in a most volatile form. It is directly derived from psychoanalysis. Alcoholics Anonymous provides a twenty-four-hour transferential figure of a specific superego kind while it exhorts the ego to stand up for itself and stop drinking. All of the other self-help movements are similarly based upon one or another analytic principle although they may deny this.

Psychotherapy of course blinded its eyes to the growing number of people who applied for help but who were not phobic, hysteric, obsessive, compulsive, schizoid, or dissociated in the usual way, but simply seemed to languish in boredom in the fluid of their attained goals and affluence. Boredom and loneliness have never been approved as respectable medical symptoms even though they have perhaps produced more suffering than all other psychic symptoms combined. The existential neurosis, so called, which the patient offered the therapist, puzzled the practitioner since the person honestly claimed to be sick yet he did not have the necessary stigmata. Some finally decided that they deserved treatment, along with the true neurotics, but found that existing techniques did not fit. These clients essentially wanted a new purpose in life, a new meaning, and a better ability to love. If they were well along in years, they wanted the existential anxiety of death somewhat eased for them.

Thus it was that the normal, the nondiseased, the psychiatric rejects, and other disaffected elements banded together under charismatic and sometimes well-trained leaders to resolve their personal dilemmas. They usually first exhausted a whole host of lesser remedies: Zen, yoga, drugs, sexual freedom, rock, meditation, humanism, and similar others. But it was principally in their common situation, in the possibilities of intimacy with each other, that the solution seemed to lie. So it was that groups of alcoholics, drug addicts, formerly marrieds, graduated neurotics, among others, banded together in a unique self-healing venture of great moment.

Therapeutic Man can no longer look to symbols of higher significance or to incarnations of deities for his fulfillment. He is squarely on his own, condemned, Sartre would say, to freedom. Enlightenment comes more by way of a pilgrimage or odyssey, that is, by experiencing, than by the revealed truths of theology or science. It must be found as Buddha found it, and every man is his own Siddhartha.

The leap into being, the total responsibility for oneself, the freedom from parental images and divineness, the failure of material substance to bring joy, all serve to produce existential anxiety. Therapeutic Man in the anguish of care and freedom first seeks a surrogate for his lost being, a psychotherapist, and then may ultimately make his way to encounter. There, freed of persuasion, shoulds and oughts, he hopes again to discover himself and the meaning of the Other.

The image of man is thus once again Homeric. This is not a throwback to history but an indication that man's evolved cortex has not made it possible for him to come to terms with himself. Homeric man is less bound by temporality and spatiality; he goes where his fate casts him, but he is also his own fate. He does not find a world; he makes it. And he has no final agenda. He sees death as a part of existence and he takes risks without fear of it.

He oppugns sublimation because it reduces the quality of his experience. He wants not to avoid conflict but to meet it head on.

Homeric man is heroic because not suiciding is the most heroic thing a person can do. The schizophrenic is the antihero of our century because he clings to his coded and autistic truths and will not validate them interpersonally. He thus lacks humanity—which is precisely the way he is treated in the state hospital.

Psychotherapy, despite its inadequacies, has been a significant social force. There are innumerably fewer repressed people in society today and children have a better chance of growing up less disabled. Indeed, the therapeutics of the day seem often to call for a modicum of repression instead of its abridgment. But catharsis as a general principle of mental health was always insufficient because few could say what was to replace the vacuum left by the disgorged substance. Extirpating a harmful complex does not automatically replace it by a more joyous mentation.

Psychotherapy is in the long run an intellectual exercise no matter how much we detest that particular term. It is divorced from life; it is not life itself. It was founded upon an ancient philosophical maxim which claimed that the more (and clarified) information one had, that is, of reality, the healthier one would be. The limitations of a total knowledge of reality as joy are now well known, and insight as the carrier of this reality is now somewhat lacking. Clients improve every day without insight. Most people never approach the deepest truths of existence in their lifetime. Encounter has a wider universality because it is not founded upon insight but upon experiencing. This often repels the intellectual. But perhaps there is more than one way of "knowing thyself." The "knowing" of the body may be as inherently important as any cognitive closure. Empathy, intuition, synchronicity, phenomenological intentionality, are considered borderline scientific phenomena, but they move mountains every day. The concept of mental health in psychiatry has lacked that intimate touch with the community which it is only now beginning to discover.

Encounter does set limits on what I have come personally to enjoy: the beauty and grace of the precise unfolding of a personality and its consequent reconstruction. It is possibly analogous to the precipitation of a crystal. But maybe we have become like Hesse's bead game players and are using our clients for aesthetic purposes. A gun as an image in a dream is a far different matter from the gun carried by a man in my last encounter group. The dream image is disadvantaged, for not only does the real gun make the bearer feel more powerful; he is more powerful. I took the gun bearer more seriously that time than I did the neighboring client who merely dreamt about a gun. I was aware that the former could reinforce his hostile feelings in a way few neurotics could and he thereby commanded my respect and attention.

Dreams are universally repressed wishes but, alas, wishes are only rarely attained. But guns do make wishes come true, as the history of man demonstrates. Wishes, ideas, and fantasy images were never intended to be the stuff of life, only its secondary accompaniments. Mathematics, for example, is only the representation of processes and never the processes themselves, but mathematicians often act as though the latter were true. Thus psychotherapy imperceptibly became a game in its own right, but the viable togetherness of the participants remains as fresh as ever. This is why the dyadic encounter overrides any theory which may be imposed on it.

Zen Buddhism has convincingly shown the aridity of the intervening concept and how it saps energy from the phenomenon proper. Psychotherapy acts similarly to abridge the naturalness of the social transaction and often becomes a barrier to humanization by a strange twist of fate. Encounter synthesizes id, ego, and superego while minimizing the intervening conceptual act, just as a hysterical conversion experience fuses and cements in an instant without awareness. Encounter, of course, overstresses the direct experience; but then, all reformations go too far.

All contemporary therapeutic systems are based on Freud. His discoveries and a century of hard-won victories in psychiatry cannot be disregarded. But it is important to understand that growth is a process of converting the biological organism to a humanistic one. Becoming a joyous adult means that one must learn to transcend reflexes, instincts, drives, and biological programming for beauty, hope, tenderness, love, and compassion. One is not toilet-trained to void waste; voiding happens regardless of training. A child is toilet-trained because fecal vulgarity is offensive to human dignity. Social training is therefore a process of becoming a person with suitably refined sensibilities.

Now no one would seriously quarrel with this thesis except that it is observed more in the breach than in the doing. Mothers equate humanness in children with weakness and femininity. They are fearful and guilty about tenderness. Powerlessness is a danger, and the humanized person is above all powerless. *Caveat emptor* (in the market place) means that humanity should be left at home commercially. Parents limit sensitivity, awareness, and bodily feeling, and they very carefully circumscribe the child's experiences. This is not so much a lack of basic trust as a covert conspiracy to reduce ecstasy to their own level of experience. Normative books on child development become best sellers because mothers want more to be confirmed in their child development beliefs than to be freed from them. They want fruitful, happy children, but strictly within the mold of their own superego.

Thus it is that the person grows up feeling that he has dislocated parts of himself somewhere. Just as long as he is goal-directed, he can defend himself. But eventually he begins a search for the missing parts and will attach himself to anyone who offers to show him "the way." These missing parts I interpret as some of the component selves that make up the total self. Transference is in one sense not so much the reinstatement of parental models as the opportunity to recover the lost selves under proper aegis. Whatever is missing in the personality drains energy until it is found and reconciled with the totality of self.

When one inquires as to just what these lost selves might be, it turns out that they are certain experiences which have vital representation in consciousness. Deprived, mutilated, neurotic, or psychotic children miss certain poignant experiences which are critical to their growth. A female client of mine had never masturbated in her life, not because it was expressly forbidden by her parents, but because it did not fit into the context of her family living. As an adult woman she missed this area of experience, to know her own sexual and bodily response possibilities better, "openness to fucking," she called it, and set out to recover it by masturbating profusely although she had any of a number of men friends who served adequately. Encounter works experientially because the missed subself, the unexperienced, is experienced with one or several group members who represent that subself which has been missed. That is to say that the encounter experience makes up for both the inadequate introject and the false one. It is the call to reexperience.

Encounter represents existentialism—the philosophy of the human condition—carried into the corpus of society. Political existentialism, having shown itself inadequate to deal with the problems of the corporate state and dehumanizing affluence, reverted back to individual forms for social solutions.[15] Encounter is the extremest form of the individual activist position, which counters Hegelian metapsychology. But it is questionable whether even Heidegger in his philosophic correction for man intended us to go this far. He apparently believed in the embodiment of personal forces—of care—in the symbols of the state. Rationalism and idealism, historical philosophical positions, as an approach to personal identity or a personal philosophy of life, look less and less appealing today. But we are not on the other hand yet finished with romanticism.

Existential psychiatry, stressing the phenomenology of the person, and the meaning of the existing moment, delimited the history of the person. Binswanger's ahistorical approach to Ellen West[16] shocked the classically-trained psychotherapist because the chain of causation from infancy to her neurosis was ignored. It was set aside, so to speak, for the way Ellen West experienced her world and her decision to be in it in a specific way. But psychotherapy was reluctant to substitute what it considered drama for causation, and Miss West's ultimate suicide all but decided against clinical phenomenology and existential psychiatry.

In retrospect, Binswanger's approach to Ellen West was not bad therapy at all. He made it possible for the patient to con-

[15] Marcuse, H. *Negations—Essays in Critical Theory* (trans. by J. J. Shapiro). Boston: Beacon Press, 1968.

[16] Binswanger, L. "The Case of Ellen West," in R. May (Ed.) *Existence*. New York: Basic Books, 1958.

sciously choose her fate, which is in a sense all that any of us can do. The specific American thanatophobia interprets the death of the client as the supreme failure of melioration; but not living the only life one has can be much worse. Legions of people want to be divorced, change jobs, alter their appearance, be female instead of male, white instead of black, and even want to conclude their existence but cannot. Any therapeutic mode which permits growth in full continuity of life, and as an outcome of sober and realistic reflection, is a satisfactory therapeutic medium.

The drag of the past is receding as an influence on the present and even the most traditional psychoanalyst does not subscribe to the theory of the infantile genesis of the neurosis in the same way he did when he was trained. The ego has assumed its rightful place. The client today forces an emphasis upon his phenomenological situation, relatively ignores his specific neurotic symptoms, and will not be put off by analytical interpretations alone.

Existentialism and phenomenology brought consciousness back into the center focus of being. We had become supremely enthralled by the unconscious, and the death instinct naturally became its chief manifestation.[17] Those of us who daily work with the unconscious do not minimize its benefits and even its beauty. But I think we misjudged the laws of the unconscious and the way it makes its contribution to life. Opening the psychic Pandora's Box was not really as difficult as expected, and its structured relationship to the preconscious and conscious was not as elemental as Freud posited. The unconscious not only deals in illegal traffic between itself and consciousness, but involves every single act of behavior, which it influences by virtue of its dynamic force. A ship proceeds by way of its hull even though the hull is under water and cannot be seen.

Phenomenology and Gestalt psychology proved not only the unity and wholeness of the percept, but a certain phenomenological intentionality or tension on the part of the organism to proceed in certain ways. In every perception the unconscious as well as the

---

[17] Brown, N. O. *Love's Body.* New York: Random House, 1966.

conscious participated, but the former represented the intention while the latter was the awareness or choice-aspect of that specific intention. Consciousness is election. Election is not so much diminished by repression as it is by a total life-design which is not ego-syntonic with the person himself. Why does catharsis so often seem brilliantly effective while leaving the client still fixed to his neurotic behavior?

Encounter makes few distinctions between conscious and unconscious, and while it recognizes human conflict and its anxiety-producing properties, it maintains that a person has a choice of either keeping or discarding a symptom once he establishes the fact that the symptom blocks his fulfillment. The peak moments of transcendence and beauty in experience always involve intimacy, sensitivity, joy, and personal encounter in some way. Even misery bands people joyously together and seeks in its common plight to reinstate itself. Eastern religions, through their Western practitioners, along with existential philosophy, finally moved those persons who were formerly reconciled to themselves to sharpen their sensibilities, their intuitive and meditative capacities, their body responses, their awareness, their loving feelings, by meeting and discussing their status with each other. The members of encounter groups thus seek their own hegemony and set their own conditions of growth. There is therefore some natural antipathy between those who go to encounter groups and those who lie supine on the couch.

Therapeutic Man now sometimes sees the vision of a new personal and social freedom through encounter. This is the promise of finding once again his own subjectivity and a communitas now in limbo. But encounter is not meant by them to be a psychic treatment modality but rather a means of humanizing the dehumanized in marriage, work, recreation, education,[18] and even melioration.

The fact that encounter is potentially so pregnant does not alter the fact that in practice it leaves much to be desired. Like all

[18] A prime example of the extension of encounter to education is seen in the new Johnson College of the University of Redlands (California). Traditional methods of learning take second place to encounter as the medium of emotional and attitudinal learning in all areas of knowledge.

new growth movements it attracts the opportunist, the promoter, the self-styled healer, the charismatic would-be saint, the sick, and even the sadistic. It also appeals to those people who cannot survive creatively without the amniotic fluid of a coterie and who find nothing in their aloneness. They go to encounter groups like some go to Arthur Murray clubs. My attempt to uncover follow-ups which have been made of encounter group experiences have been nil.[19] The evidence therefore in its favor at this date consists simply of testimonials.

The principal deficiency in encounter for me is that it lacks a theory. It borrows precisely from that medical model which it oppugns, and from yoga,[20] which anticipated it for millennia. In logically ordering its working hypotheses it falls all over itself with the baubles and bangles of meditation, introspection, lowering sensory thresholds, deep breathing, orgastic response, physical exercise, fantasy experience, touching, nudity, and other manifestations of preciousness.[21] It competes in the marketplace with the psychiatrist, John Robert Powers, Maharishi Mahesh Yogi, Dale Carnegie, rapid reading, rock, Alan Watts, and pot, for liberation.

Encounter has not yet gotten around to specifying its dangers, and it ignores those who have been hurt by it and even suicided. Encounter says nothing at all about marginal encounter groups which have no encounter at all in them. It often proclaims a universal panacea like any other quack nostrum foisted on the public.

Encounter is perhaps still too young to have an ethic. Presumably its leaders are guided by whatever ethics they bring to encounter, whether theology, psychology, social work, management, psychiatry, law, or art. Some encounter leaders are teachers, artists, businessmen, visionaries, and self-healed laymen, all without formal

---

[19] Since writing this, I have received word from William Schutz that 80 per cent of his clients have reported tangible benefits from their encounter group experience with him.

[20] Eliade, M. *Yoga—Immortality and Freedom* (second edition) Princeton: Princeton University Press, 1969.

[21] See, for example, Schutz, W. C. *Joy—Expanding Human Awareness*. New York: Grove Press, 1967; and Gunther, B. *Sense Relaxation Below Your Mind*. New York: Collier, 1968.

professional ethical indoctrination. And the psychedelic drug movement has been uncomfortably close to some of the larger encounter
centers.

It is true that some encounter leaders are trained psychotherapists,[22] but a number of them have themselves become disillusioned with psychotherapy and are hostile toward it. None of
them, as far as I know, believe this to be evidence of the need for
more personal analysis on their part. Others legitimately believe
that the psychotherapeutic well has run dry, and that a new source
of healing and growth is needed. They are looking sincerely for a
new theory of man—and a concomitant practice to humanize him.
Others cannot meet the professional standards of clinical practice
but nevertheless feel a calling to help people. A kind of anarchy
takes over in which the leader with the greatest charisma, and perhaps the most diversified "awakening" techniques, is most desired
and has the greatest following. Each leader builds a personal following by collecting testimonials and quickly forgets his obligation to
science. While industry has set some standards for its human relations consultants, the broader exponents of encounter have not
and do not promise to do so. I predict that in the decade ahead
encounter leaders will require certification or licensing by the state
once the evils have accumulated sufficiently to arouse public
response.

The marathon encounter experience, as a special form of
encounter, seems to imply that intensity and forced confrontation is
an important factor in growth. The term marathon, from the efforts
of the Hellenic messenger who brought news of the battle of Marathon, implies seeing things to a conclusion regardless of the consequences, and this fits the American temperament. The marathon
encounter, by the bye, is also very lucrative for the group leader
and often goes along with his usually insistent temperament. But
the principle of spaced learning still applies to growth experiences
and we know that much occurs between treatment sessions. Marathon encounter seems at present a hysterical form of encounter.

[22] *The Berkeley Barb,* an "underground newspaper," regularly carries
in its classified advertisements listings for at least a dozen encounter groups
for whom members are sought.

Psychotherapists give much attention to whom they accept for treatment. Encounter accepts everyone who applies and even solicits for customers. The assumption is that everyone is capable of having an encounter. But we know that it is precisely because people cannot encounter that they come to encounter groups. Many such applicants have lost meaning in their lives or are depressed about life. Others are schizoid, or even ambulatory schizophrenic, and some clinically neurotic. Some seek only to recover a lost artistry or creativity. And, of course, the young and socially disaffected are there, as well as the nondiseased.

It might be claimed that encounter can do no harm. But I have clients who have gone from one encounter group to another and have finally ended up in dyadic psychotherapy where they finally improved. They also needed the healing encounter, but transferential matters preempted their self so that the dyadic encounter had to come first.

Psychotherapy and encounter have more or less spurned each other as conjoint approaches. But individual and group approaches to growth and healing are not by any means antithetical. The question then becomes one of how encountering is to be used for the total good of the client. In my own practice I have kept dyadic psychotherapy clients out of my encounter groups, and my encounter group members out of my dyadic psychotherapy.[23] But I am not exactly certain why. I have a deep and queasy feeling that as things stand they are opposed to each other. I have been rebuffed in encounter groups for trying to be the therapist and have indeed learned the error of my ways. But I do know they belong together, and I can now only see encounter essentially as a variant of psychotherapy to be done only by people trained in psychotherapeutic method. This is, of course, one of my unresolved disparities.

All of the above shortcomings are, of course, the growing

---

[23] I consider most group therapies which operate in a medical framework as laboring under the same limitations as classical psychotherapy. There are of course exceptions. The differences involve the function of the encounter leader, the theory under which the encounter takes place, and the methodology employed to induce the encounter.

pains of a possibly new structure in society. Their solutions can be expected when a theory of Encounter becomes clear. But it seems at any rate true that the base of psychotherapy has now been broadened and that psychotherapy is no longer merely for the sick. The benefits of creativity and freedom, through the discoveries of Freud, are for all who want to partake of them—and encounter will help to make them possible.

II

Therapeutic Relationships in Groups

Bertram R. Forer

Homo sapiens is the most intelligent of animals and the most ingenious in self-destruction. The process of converting him into a human being provides a complex continuity to his life and creates a new domain of problems. He now has to contend not only with the biological requirements for his survival, but more problematically with the fact of psychological structure, personality, and socialized human nature.

Biologically natural activities have been curbed and re-directed not by the predictable pressures of a physical world, but by the less predictable, more variable, somewhat capricious, and partially consistent demands of a social world. The significance of external physical events in shaping him is subordinated to the preoccupation with relationships to other persons, real or fantasied, external or internalized. When he has acquired human nature, his potentialities increase enormously and his limits are set by his early history. He has created within himself an internal structure which represents his adaptations to early human relationships. And this structure in its most obvious expressions is what he experiences as himself and what others define him to be. He has acquired attach-ments and antipathies to other human beings whose power has forced him to differentiate and subdivide himself, to accept and communicate to others some selected aspects of what has been built into him, and to reject, disenfranchise, hide, or repress other aspects. He has, then, built a structure whose purposes include segregation of sectors of himself against imagined possibilities of being destroyed, punished, or excluded by other persons, or being made to feel anxiety or painful guilt—which are internal substitutes for others' reactions.

The fact of his structuring indicates that he has relinquished some freedom to experience, wish, and act in order to maintain continuity, recognizability, stability, and predictability and in order to insure continuing relationshps with important persons. Self-maintenance and relationship maintenance are both essential to life but are often at odds. He has become a person whose sense of self, whatever it has happened to be, is his most important possession and often his most threatened one. A major issue in his life, then, has to be how to maintain the sense of self through the sequential events of his life, both directing the course of life and dealing with uncontrollable assaults and repercussions, and at the same time re-tain other persons. For there are continual threats to the continuity of the experience of self and to successful accomplishment of those activities and relationships that represent the expression of self.

Since the world around him changes, he must continually take into account the persons, the opportunities for the activities which he seeks or is required to live out, in his physical status and in his personal capacities, and he must continually change himself and his activities in accordance with them. If, to maintain an integrated view of himself, he is unable to readapt to changed internal or external circumstances, his capacity to function flexibly is diminished and he is at the mercy of those changes. If, on the other hand, concern with adapting to externals has excessive priority over the demands of his idiosyncratic nature, he renounces his integrity as a unique person and is unable to create for himself a meaningful continuity or direction in his life. There is, then, a dilemma between relinquishing some parts of one's structured self in order to cope with change and maintaining a rigid, impenetrable stance which disregards the reality of changes and achieves a deceptive stability. Somewhere, perhaps oscillating between these two extremes, lies the kind of adaptiveness with integration that enables psychological growth, the encompassing of external changes by means of internal changes that add to rather than detract from the experience of self.

It has been a complex process by which the humanity of *Homo sapiens* has developed, but it is an equally difficult and complex process to maintain and nourish the individual's humanity through phases of development throughout life. And, like the initial process of humanization, the maintenance of personal humanity requires other human beings.

The evidence from studies on sensory deprivation, both anecdotal and experimental, is that the human being whose nature is not continually reinforced by other persons loses at least temporarily some of his most complex psychological abilities. In more subtle ways clients who seek psychotherapy manifest self-imposed sensory deprivations through the interposition of barriers against the humanity-reinforcing effects of other persons: they intentionally deprive themselves of social stimulation which is potentially ego-building and integrative. The most blatant are those whom we label schizophrenics. Characteristically they internalize inconsistent, self-destructive features of their early human relationships and, in their need to protect their primitive selves from further disruption, they withdraw from participation in the more complex, mature aspects of the humanization process and settle for incomplete humanization. They accept incomplete psychological structure to avoid threatened dissolution of whatever structural features they have achieved. Their basic distrust communicates the message that they refuse to internalize any more of other persons. In a very real sense they are almost completely dominated by their histories and are virtually incapable of achieving a future.

Adult relationships have two supplementary functions that are sometimes in destructive opposition to each other. The primordial function is self-maintenance. One uses stable relationships with other persons to reinforce one's feeling of identity, in a sense to provide a constancy, both cognitive and affective, in the environment within which the need to change is minimized, and complacency about oneself is maximized. In the extreme position a relationship is clung to in order to forestall change, with its concomitant anxiety, even change that might seem to be gratifying and sought after. While the person may express rage at the frustrating quality of the relationship, he refuses to change it, even in the direction of improvement—most likely because the change in itself is temporarily disruptive or disintegrative. This kind of stance involves rejection of new experience, selective pursuit of those who will reinforce the current state of affairs and the careful, although unconscious, training of other persons to react to him in his accustomed views of himself. He uses other persons as mirrors or as marionettes whom he rejects when they show idiosyncratic attitudes toward him.

The other function of human relationships is to provide within the framework of social acceptance new experiences that include reassessment of self and encouragement for the rediscovery of formerly abandoned or repressed structures of the self. This process, essential to growth, might be called social nourishment. The failure of many marriages and the waning of other relationships sometimes represent the failure to obtain social nourishment from the other person, resistance to incorporation of what might have been available, or the protective selection of a person whose function is to reinforce the same kind of self-repression that was brought into the relationship, thus a replica of the internal structures which led to the original self-disavowal. In other instances relationships terminate when they have been mutually nourishing up to the point of the personal limitations of one or both persons. If both have grown, the relationship should be considered a success despite its termination.

Psychological growth as a continuous process throughout life presupposes first of all that one be reasonably well humanized, that one has built into psychological structures some ways of experiencing, thinking, feeling, and acting that have validity for the social group in which one was created. The question of how much growth and its rapidity will depend upon the variety of internalized human experiences, the degree of availability or, conversely, repression of substructures. The selective repression characteristic of most persons implies a state of affairs much like that of the multiple personality. The degree of repression or of tolerance for internal diversity will determine capacity for change and flexibility and the degree of adaptability (ability to obtain nourishment from) to alien groups or persons, hence will determine the degree of freedom to participate in a variety of environments.

To incorporate into the self a narrow spectrum of human relationships can limit the degree to which growth is possible and the kinds of environments within which one can function. To incorporate structurally into oneself ineffective representatives of the world at large who themselves were unable to grow or adapt may create a person with minimal resources for coping with the rest of his world or whose internal structure is fragmented and unintegrated under a reasonably consistent experience of self. Many schizophrenics, for example, have incorporated such faulty and unpredictable specimens of social reinforcement that they are forced to devote too much effort trying to achieve harmony among the half-humanized fragments of self-structure and cannot find the energy, resources, or courage to deal with the real persons in their adult environments. Their incomplete humanization differs radically from that of children because it includes resistance to the social nourishment and concomitant social and self-exploration that are essential to subsequent steps in humanization.

The one antidote to their endless attempt to master, survive, or escape from the internalized quasi-human parent structure is through intimate, perhaps symbiotic, involvement with another person. The developmental tragedy is that the noxious influence of early persons has built in such distrust of other persons and terror at the thought of permitting further psychic penetration that survival seems to demand withdrawal into a closed system. But a closed system that has built-in self-destructive features is doomed. Its goal is not growth, self-expression, or gratification, but retreat from itself. In some measure and in some psychological areas this kind of resistance is true of almost everyone. Those who are incompletely humanized are nonetheless addicted to human relationships and pathologically fearful of the next steps that they must take to become more fully human. Thus their relationships are largely or entirely dominated by the early persons in their lives whose images, injunctions and anti-self qualities persist internally and blot out perception of others.

The less disturbed and even the reasonably mature are caught in a similar though less pervasive dilemma. To grow, their egos must be continually expanded by new interpersonal experiences. Yet, for the majority, the internalized parents in the form of taboos and requirements dictate the terms of self-attitudes that conflict with the realities of adult relationships.

In the process of internalizing parental influences the child turns against parts of himself with feelings of shame and guilt and literally dissociates them, structures what is acceptable in himself as if continually struggling to please the parents who are setting rules of conduct. To disobey is to court disapproval, loss of love, abandonment, annihilation. What is repressed or dissociated as the not-self becomes an obstacle to other human relationships because it is isolated from the rest of the self by feelings of disapproval which are projected onto others, even onto those who express approval. The obstacle takes the double form of enacting roles that were learned as adaptations to parents and are inappropriate to adult relationships on the one hand and energetically hiding from others those parts of the self which have been renounced as incongruous with how one is supposed to be. This is a crucial determinant of alienation among persons that guarantees loneliness even in the presence of others. Since the self is split, the portion that is renounced can never experience love, admiration, acceptance. It can experience only the self-imposed rejection. Hence, as long as it is dissociated any evidence of love or acceptance is distrusted or not perceived at all. As long as some of the self-feeling is locked in with the rejected self-structure, the self is minimally nourishable or modifiable. Accomplishments are experienced as unrewarding for more than a moment and negative concepts of the self persist, unreachable by evidence. Approval may be felt as acceptance for self-renunciation or one's acting ability. A relevant analogy is that of the hidden puppeteer whose puppets are patted or stroked. The puppeteer may observe the approval, but his skin cannot feel it. For personal relationships to change internal structure, the structures must be discernible and in direct contact with self-feeling and other persons.

From this structural-interpersonalistic view the client who seeks therapy is someone who seeks nourishment from someone even while rejecting it. He has not learned how to obtain it, perceive it or utilize it. He has, in fact, learned a variety of ways of preventing it. While he may say with anguish that he needs love, he is ingenious at turning it away. While he may believe that he is asking for something from others and that he is communicating with them, he is likely to be primarily involved in a dialogue between parts of himself which are experienced as other external persons. He does not know how out of contact with others he really is, how much he is living in an internal world which he projects onto those with whom he is presumably involved. These are among the major issues that must be dealt with in both individual and group therapeutic relationships.

It is rare for the new client truly to present himself to others. Most commonly he presents his standards, the images that he believes he must live up to, or the compromise roles he has learned to enact to meet internalized standards, or his self-disapproval for not being able to live up to these standards. Latent communications frequently take the following forms: (1) You should like the me that is self-depriving. (2) If you cannot like the terrible person I say that I am, perhaps you can admire me for having such high standards and for condemning myself so properly. (3) I hate people because I know they cannot love the parts of me that I hate.

In group psychotherapy, with the help of group members, the therapist can see that while his clients say they wish to relate intimately with one another, their behavior says the opposite: that is the one thing they do not intend to do—reveal their hidden selves. But until they do, all feelings of intimacy are bogus, a cheap thrill. They seek to obtain love from one another for their cover stories and old adaptations and do not dare to seek love in the areas of the dissociated parts of themselves. Yet it is the "bad child" who needs the love and not the "good" one. The games they play, the masks they wear, the scripts they quote repetitiously are impersonal ritualistic responses to the family in their heads, who are surrogates for other real persons. The misperceptions of others, which we call transference, are externalizations of their own internal populations. We soon detect that they are not talking to each other. They are talking to themselves. They hear others largely when others say what they already believe of themselves. They are maintaining their self-structures by remaining self-contained, relating to inner rather than outer persons. Their puppets dance together while the puppeteers remain hidden behind the scenes.

An important question about group encounters is the amount of lasting effect derived from what may appear to be an intense emotional experience. No doubt many participants in brief, concentrated encounter situations are significantly changed structurally by such experiences. Many—too many—are not. In subsequent follow-up it is apparent that the emotional effects have faded away as though they had had a thrill and remembered having had it. But their human relationships and their self-conceptions remain placidly unbudged. It is not the intensity alone of the emotional interaction that counts, but what internally is involved in the encounter. Many clients in groups have had much individual therapy, even complete psychoanalyses, and have attained much insight, yet made minimal structural change. This fact and the subsequent desperation of both therapists and clients may be an important determinant of the recent proliferation of both gimmicks and creative innovations in group therapy.

In summary, our view is that human problems represent a premature disruption of the process of humanization which involves the following aspects: (1) substitution of fantasy persons for real persons in both communication and emotional involvement; (2) dissociation of parts of the self which are interlocked with internal representations of early significant persons; (3) presentation of self in terms of compromise adaptations to these internalized human relationships; and (4) reluctance to reopen dissociated parts of the self to awareness and to current human relationships. Therefore, the therapeutic process can be viewed not as treatment but as resumption of the humanizing or psychological growth process where it had been blocked off, reexperiencing dissociated parts of the self, converting structures to flexible exploratory human relationships, redefining self through current relationships.

The philosophy of encounter groups, though poorly grounded in personality theory, has accentuated some of these points. The focus is upon immediate experience of self with others in an open emotional relationship. This emphasis represents an important part of what is lacking in the more orthodox varieties of psychoanalytic method.

The orthodox prosecution of long-term psychoanalysis can have the effect of substituting for the stunting of humanization another more benevolent yet somewhat constraining system, sometimes a superego system, but at least a theoretical system based upon identification with the psychoanalytic model or procedure. The injunction might be "You are bad, you are resisting," or "What you say is always a cover-up; you are hiding the true meanings." Such an approach is limited in its possibilities for providing new experiences of self in a fluid, mutually penetrating relationship. Historically a crucial contribution of the psychoanalytic relationship has been the impartiality and impersonality of the therapist. While the objectivity of this stance is of evident corrective value, its limitation lies in the area of omitting new kinds of relating with other persons with emotional responses from the others. The analyst's needs are hidden. But it is necessary for growth that the client make contact with other persons' needs as well as his own. Identification with the analyst's position is not the same as obtaining some emotional nourishment from the therapist and other persons which can liberate and expand what is present and dissociated in the client. Something new has to be added: what was missed by too early protective retreat from involvements with real persons. Objectivity is not enough. Exposure of the transference neurosis does not necessarily promulgate freedom to grow continually. And insight does not necessarily change one's behavior and manner of relating to others.

But it can be too cheap a solution to expect momentary intimacies in short-term contacts or forced activities without awareness of inner structures to solve the problem. Encounters must become internalized and integrated and old adaptations must be undone to produce enduring structural modifications. The danger is that they also become dissociated or isolated.

With current emphases spotlighting the therapeutic role of the relationship between clients and therapists, the role of the therapist needs clarification. If the therapist views his role largely as a refined use of technical skills, he is likely to reinforce his clients' use of words as a means of hiding themselves and maintaining the status quo. To become a therapist requires a form of adaptation which *pretends* to relationships as a clever, socially-rewarded method of helping others while being largely unaffected by them. Too often therapists use their work as a surrogate for human relationships and to avoid recognition of their own developmental failures. They can use the relationship as a means of furthering their own growth.

Despite the vast differences among therapists as persons, differences that are inevitable and valuable, there is one major attitudinal contribution which they all have to make to their clients: their indications of humanity, which include their feelings of disapproval for their clients' self-renunciation and their encouragement and reinforcement of self-expression and resumption of growth struggles.

Since a basic aspect of the process of humanization commits the person to preoccupation with human relationships, the initial and persistent leverage for growth will lie in the client's need to get something from the therapist and the group. The more he is aware of this need, the more he is forced to challenge his old views, to confront the dilemma of relating to internal fantasy persons versus relating to group members. And the kinds of needs involved here are less likely to be based upon biological drives than upon structural requirements. As the group progresses over time in its relatedness, group members become more and more valued and begin to challenge or replace such internalized persons as superego introjects.

It is inevitable that members present themselves in those terms that are available to them at the moment, ready-made roles or stances. The therapist can immediately and persistently point out that these are covers over the real person inside, that they all have apprehensions about revealing what they are really like, that they view self-revelation as exposure rather than self-expression, that their first communications are largely protective and in reality unnecessary. They need to be shown that what they have to offer each other is not the conformist methods they have learned in order to get along, but the more private aspects of themselves. To confront or assault for game-playing is not necessarily therapeutic because on one hand being attacked is an important part of their form of adaptation and on the other hand they do not know what part of themselves is being attacked. They, themselves, have not yet learned to discriminate between adaptations to the superego, or the superego itself, and their dissociated selves. It can be helpful for the therapist to inform them when they are revealing principles or rules or anti-selves rather than selves, that they are speaking from the position of guilt or parental introjects rather than from their own selves. This kind of communication is particularly important when the client is condemning himself for some symptomatic act such as being late or overeating, which the therapist has to recognize not as unacceptable behavior or resistance but rather as an abortive expression of a valuable but dissociated part of the self that requires liberation, not punishment. The intent here is to create an atmosphere of accepting the unexpressed, dissociated self and allying with it against the internalized oppositions to it. Concurrently they

can become aware that their living in terms of internalized standards deprives other persons as well as themselves, just as they become aware of being deprived by others who relate from the position of virtue, rules, or other impersonal principles. Groups learn
rather quickly that saying what they "should" say is not relating
to other persons at all.

They do not need to know the unconscious significance of
all of their associations or eruptions other than to recognize how
they avoid deep contact with themselves and one another, through
selective hearing, transference misperception, rejection of approval,
as if they are reacting to fantasies of one another, fantasies that
they have for a long time lived by. To become preoccupied with
unconscious meanings in itself can be used primarily to distance
others. Resistances can be viewed not as bad behavior, but as protection against introjects and self-frustrating rejection of nourishment from other persons. Their loneliness they can learn to
recognize as *entirely* self-imposed, because they will see in others
as well as themselves how little they dare to take from others into
the lonely parts of themselves.

The affects of anxiety, shame, and guilt are described as
emotional reactions to internal personages that essentially alienate
them from the nourishing influences of group members. They are
motives for not expressing something in their real selves lest they
receive the same negative responses which they formerly received
or imagined receiving. Such feelings are essentially self-reinforcers
of the narcissistic retreat from other persons and they can mark
critical turning points when they emerge in the group. The old
adaptation is to renounce the part of the self that threatens to break
through. The growth-engendering process is to override the counter-
feeling and once again, or for the first time, reveal the self-fragment
to other persons. This therapeutic crisis arises when parts of the
self become unrepressed, stimulated by an extra-group experience
or the impact of someone in the group itself. The struggle against
shame, guilt, and anxiety out of past relationships contains such
elements as these:

1. They maintain loneliness and hiddenness because they
are convinced that they will be disapproved of for this unacceptable

part of themselves. They can experience their walling-off from others.

2. They recognize that this part of themselves is inescapable despite their need to oppose it.

3. They realize that they cannot feel loved as long as this part of them with its conditioned opposition exists within them. Whatever approval they receive is contaminated by the feeling that the unspoken self will still be rejected.

4. Their holding back is a capitulation to the position of the internal enemy of the self, the superego, the disapproving parents.

5. They recognize or experience an identity between the attitudes of the internal persons and the group members.

At this point it is possible to effect a structural change. Sharing of this dissociated part of the self with the group under such emotional conditions is an abreaction of original crises that aborted the process of development, a reliving of the process of internalization of social disapproval, a reexperiencing of the intro-ject as coming from the inside and as an external projection. But it is accomplished with new persons who, hopefully, compete with the orginal introject, express a different attitude to the newly exposed part of the self, and become discernibly different from the introject. The past and the present are brought face to face and the past renounced. What happens structurally is a replacement of the introjected critical attitudes by benevolent group feelings, and a shift in locus of identification from the superego or fantasy-other toward identification with the formerly renounced part of the self. There is likely over time a sequence of stages in this shift from a feeling of confession through partial tolerance to enjoyment and even pride in connection with the dissociated part of the self.

For significant changes to occur, the following processes seem important:

Dissociation. The client must experience the dissociated part of himself and simultaneously the shame, guilt, or anxiety related to the expected disapproval. In addition he must experience or be helped to experience his fantasy expectations, which are, of course, a projection of the internalized parents onto the group.

Feedback. The client must receive from the therapist and the group a kind of feedback different from what his internal parent tells him. He may not for a time even hear what the group says that may be contrary to his expectations.

Reality-testing. The client cannot easily take into himself the emotional impact of this experience, which is so out of congruence with the way he has taught himself to structure the world. An important activity of the therapist at this point is to force the client to verbalize expectations, his own self-condemnations, the group's responses, particularly to hear the latter. The therapist may insist that the client ask group members how they feel about him, that he perceive the discrepancy, that he take the group seriously.

Reinforcement. Both therapist and group can use their power to convince the client that the newly exposed part of himself is not so bad or even desirable and that his sharing of that part of himself with them was experienced by them as good, giving, loving, certainly more acceptable than the cover-up maneuvers. To be rewarded for behavior that was thought punishable forces reassessment of self and in fact adds to the experience and breadth of the self.

This process is different from insight, though insight may be included. It involves reliving of feeling and experience, but it adds the dimensions of new, albeit tentative, behaviors and feelings along with experiencing of new kinds of response from other persons. Having experienced the positively-reinforcing feedback from others, the client becomes less devoted to using others for self-maintenance of maladaptive defensive roles and begins to experience gratification from human relationships. Loneliness lessens and openness increases. Love seems a possibility. Other persons become less threatening as possible critics and begin to seem valuable. It may be safe to take from them, to let them get under one's skin. He begins to realize how he had trained others to reject part of him as he, himself, had been doing; that what had turned others off was not his inner self, but his methods for hiding it. He begins to accept that what is precious about him is not his good behavior, his niceness, his suffering, but his unique humanness and his pursuit of its expression, that the voices of guilt and shame are the voices of his introjects and not his person.

One mechanism that has been implied up to this point, but not specified, is that of introjection. The client has taken into himself structurally some aspects of civilization in the form of parental attitudes, some of them opposed to parts of himself. What makes a structural difference in him and fosters resumption of the humanizing process is elimination of some introjects and his defenses against them and reopening himself psychologically to the process of introjection. Intimate relationships with others always involve introjecting something from the other person into some area of the self, preferably into the area experienced and liked as self and not into the area of opposing critical figures such as the superego. When the client truly experiences approval and affection from others for the newly reopened parts of himself, he has in fact introjected new social nourishment which does not add a foreign element to him, but which, rather, revalidates what was latent inside himself, but unused. When this has occurred, he has through reacceptance of the risks of vulnerability reopened himself to living and loving with others in the present real world.

III

Role Freedom in a TORI Group

Jack R. Gibb, Lorraine M. Gibb

Persons, groups, and organizations are living organisms that grow. Such growth is a directional movement from fear to trust, from restricted to open communication, from imposition to self-determination, and from dependence to interdependence. All social organisms have a potential for growth that has apparently been greatly underestimated. The rate of growth is greatly variable. Growth may come in spurts, periods of gradual movement, or latent periods which show little visible evidence of change. The determiners of growth direction and growth potential are largely internal to the system, but the determiners of growth rate seem to be in the interpersonal environment of the organism. Recent studies suggest that both the macroenvironment and the immediate primary group environment are powerful determiners of growth.

Summarized in Table 1 is a theory of growth that is described in detail elsewhere.[1] The central dynamic of the growth process is a movement from fear to trust. Latent fear predisposes individuals to build social structures around role relations, develop strategies for mask maintenance, attempt to manage motivations by various forms of persuasion, and maintain tight control systems. The individual camouflages his fears to himself by building role barricades; he camouflages his humanness with an idealized presenting self; he reacts to imposed motivations by attempting to impose motivations on others; and he protects himself from intimacy by depending or rebelling. With experience in high trust environments, however, he tends to be more personal; he replaces facades with intimacy and directness; he becomes more search-oriented and self-determining; and he develops the capacity for making interdependent relationships with relevant and significant others.

The development of a small group follows an analogous course. In early periods of group life the theme is latent and disguised fear. Relations are primarily role relations; interpersonal commerce is carried on in polite terms that mask an interpersonal underworld of covert strategy; members buy and sell advice and affection; and controls are formalized and necessary. As groups grow, they reduce fears and build a climate of increased trust, an open feedback system, a norm of joint inquiry and common goal setting, and the free interplay of emerging norms. Analogous sequences are seen in organizational life, though the patterns are much more complicated and imbedded.[2]

Recent evidence suggests that the small group experience can powerfully facilitate this growth process. Individuals can learn to alter both their own growth rates and the group and institutional environment in which they live.[3] This ability can be developed in

[1] Gibb, J. R., and Gibb, L. M. "Humanistic Elements in Group Growth." In J. F. T. Bugental (Ed.), *Challenges of Humanistic Psychology.* New York: McGraw-Hill, 1967.

[2] Gibb, J. R. "Fear and Facade: Defensive Management." In R. E. Farson (Ed.), *Science and Human Affairs.* Palo Alto: Science and Behavior Books, 1965.

[3] Gibb, J. R. "Effects of Human Relations Training." In A. E. Bergin

an intensive small group experience in which a person experiences his own change, and learns for himself that he can feel free and powerful in a significant small group.

TORI (Trust - Openness - Realization - Interdependence) theory implies that the major barriers to growth are fears and distrusts and invalid life theories that rationalize these fears and

Table 1

DIRECTIONS OF GROWTH

Critical aspects of growth	*Growth is movement from:*	*Growth is movement toward:*
Climate (Membership)	Fear-distrust role-role relations defending against evaluating formalizing rewarding, punishing	Trust-acceptance person-person relations engaging with allowing, enjoying informalizing expressing feelings
Data flow (Decision making)	Distance-facade withdrawal strategy, gamesmanship politeness, propriety masking, camouflage presenting ideal self	Openness-intimacy confrontation, fighting open influence directness, candor unmasking, showing presenting real self
Goal formation (Productivity)	Persuasion-competition teaching, modelling correcting, remedying goal imposition advice giving persuading, counselling	Realization-search learning, searching growing, becoming self-determination exploring, seeking problem solving
Control (Organization)	Dependence-dominance patterning standardizing performance controlling static form control by rules	Interdependence- emergence innovation, play emerging norms emerging fluid form interdependence, absence of rules

and S. L. Garfield (Eds.), *Handbook of Psychotherapy and Behavior Change.* New York: Wiley, 1969.

distrusts. Fortunately, the propensity for growth is strong in all living organisms. People grow under a wide variety of nurturing and contra-nurturing environments. In order to change his rate of growth a person must have deep experiences that disconfirm his fears and distrusts, and he must rebuild his life theory in a way that is more congruent with his trust experiences and trust assumptions. A TORI group is designed to provide an opportunity for this fear reduction and theory building.

A TORI experience is an emergent happening, and so in one sense there are no goals of therapy or training. The theory assumes that under certain minimal conditions certain growth processes occur as an inevitable product of the interaction. The person who sets up a program of training groups has certain training goals in mind. He makes a retrospective analysis of what happens in such groups, and creates new group opportunities in the hope that such experiences will recur. In this sense, the goals of TORI training are the following:

1. Each person must have the experience of growing. It is hoped that not only will each person experience himself as growing, but will also be seen by others as growing, and will be able to create these growth conditions in himself and in his environment.

2. Each person must experience being a free and influential member of a growing and creative group. It is hoped that each person will be part of a full range of experiences in a significant group that has trauma, conflict, confrontation, euphoria, intimacy, and other aspects of growth. Particularly critical are experiences of consensual decision making, creating a consensual goal from diversity, building a climate of open and caring feedback, and being part of a rule-free interdependence.

3. Each person must have a full opportunity to try out new behaviors and feelings. It is hoped that each person will have multiple opportunities to try out ways of behaving that fit his concept of what he would like to become, to get direct and valid feedback from others on how this new behavior is experienced by them, and to make continual modifications in his new behavior under conditions that are optimal to creative growth.

4. Each person must have an opportunity to create, verbal-

ize, and test his own theory that integrates his values and his assumptions about the world. It is hoped that the new feelings of trust that inevitably emerge from these intense group experiences will force examination of central values, attitudes toward people, and the usual assumptions that arise from fear and distrust of self, the world, and other people. For some the group is a miniature laboratory in which individuals or the total group can make informal tests of hypotheses about groups, leadership, control, approval, decision making, feedback, goal setting, and other phenomena that inevitably arise in the full group experience. Life in an open and unstructured group environment is a continual search, a creation, an experiment, a challenge, and a laboratory in which the central and recurring issues of life are continually tested. These tests range in formality from unconscious group dramas to conscious and deliberate attempts to try out a hypothesis in action in the group.

5. Each person must have an opportunity to take full responsibility for his own behavior. It is hoped that each person will have several opportunities to experience the full range of pains and exhilarations that accompany taking responsibilty for his feelings, initiations, refusals, and way of living in the group. Whether or not there is a professional in the TORI group, no one takes responsibility for protecting, nurturing, teaching, or stimulating others. As the group grows, for instance, support and warmth come from emerging feelings of caring, not from a sense of responsibilities of leadership on the part of the professional.

TORI theory is a general theory of organizational management and change. It has been described in detail elsewhere.[4] The specifications regarding the small group experience grow out of a series of studies[5] in both leaderless and professional-led groups. It became increasingly clear that the behavior of the leader was a

[4] Gibb, J. R., and Gibb, L. M. "Emergence Therapy: The TORI Process in an Emergent Group." In G. M. Gazda (Ed.), *Innovations to Group Psychotherapy*. Springfield, Ill.: Thomas, 1968.

[5] Gibb, J. R. "Climate for Trust Formation." In L. P. Bradford, J. R. Gibb, and K. D. Benne (Eds.), *T-Group Theory and Laboratory Method*. New York: Wiley, 1964.

relatively less important determiner of member learnings and group development than the norms of the group itself and the norms of the macroenvironment. The conditions under which the training occurs are critical. Trying out TORI groups in a wide variety of organizational settings has led to the following statements about the technology of climate building:

The group experience is more powerful and permanent if it is imbedded in significant organizational life. An intensive small group experience is unnecessary and less important for a person who has memberships in high-growth small groups (the natural family, a management team, a planning group, a club). Training in a natural team is far more powerful than training in the heterogeneous groups that are common in group therapy and sensitivity training.

The overall macroenvironment is probably the most powerful single factor determining the effectiveness of the group experience. During the past twenty years the norm environment of several national organizations has changed so much that training groups within the organizations have changed radically in climate, tone, responsiveness, and other relevant aspects of group life. The same group of managers meeting at Esalen, in a college dormitory, or in company headquarters will respond very differently. Organizational habits and practices must change if life is to be different following group experiences. To be effective a program of group experiences must emerge as part of a total program of environmental change, aimed at management practices, organizational structure, building design, personnel policy, and total macroenvironmental growth. The organization is an organism.

The effects of the experience dissipate rapidly unless there are preparation and follow-up. Adjunctive processes of personal therapy, personality testing, organizational consulting, job enlargement, job rotation, meditation, creativity training, and vocational counseling are frequent and custom-designed accompaniments to group experiences.

The most powerful and economical time format is the marathon. The aims listed in the previous section are realistically accomplished when the group meets for seventy or eighty hours or more, over a period of perhaps four or five days. The continuous, uninterrupted person contact of the marathon is important. Groups that meet for only two hours at a session are significantly less powerful than continuous groups. More important than the time is what the people do in it, of course. What happens in the marathon is a function of the expectations and habits that come from other group memberships.

Group size is a complex variable. If a team is the group unit, then the group should contain all of the people who are on the decision-making team, usually from five to twenty people. The authors have experimented with groups which maintain face-to-face contact with as many as six hundred people. It is quite clear that we have inherited a number of myths about size, and that we have a lot to learn about it. There is some evidence, for instance, that groups of two hundred are more powerful than smaller groups in creating a climate of growth for the participants.

Nonverbal communications and relationships are so important in creating depth of intimacy and involvement that consideration must be given to fluidity of space in creating a growth environment. This fact is true in the work environment or the religious setting as well as in the training setting. TORI group experiences are more powerful when there is space to run, dance, experiment with structure and form, take group walks, try risk experiments, relate to other groups, shout, and respond to group impulses to experiment. Space, form, air, beauty, sounds, and smells are all significant parts of the macroenvironment.

Boundaries, rules, programming, role prescriptions, and other controls greatly restrict the creativity and growth potential of the group experience. Groups are inventive in circumventing boundaries, but much of this creativity is probably dysfunctional in terms of the learning aims discussed earlier. The TORI emphasis is upon freedom and emergent growth. The group is a creative experience. Groups create norms, structures, and forms, and in the process create freedoms and ways of changing norms. Changing or fighting boundaries is a necessary and important experience. The training designer must be aware that the boundary structure of the macroenvironment predetermines the content of the group to a great degree.

Training is more powerful if the group experience is thought of as a form of life and rich living rather than as a preparation for living. Talking about "when we get back to real life" is dysfunctional for both teams and heterogeneous groups. The designer should keep in mind that everything that happens in the experience is meaningful in and of itself. There is something greatly incongruent in having the therapist or training director set up everything including meal times, travel plans, recreational schedules, dress, and training format, and then tell the group to go ahead and learn to be free, interdependent, and in charge of its own life. Group members who treat the other members of the group as instruments in their own learning ("I'm practicing on you so that I can learn to be supportive to my wife") are treating the group experience as a preparation for living. Such norms are often nurtured by the people who set up the training.

The TORI theory does not program in advance any restriction on the kind of activities that go on in a group. Anything that the group comes up with, if planned or created by the group, is potentially significant: lectures, discussions, field trips, movies, tape listening, recreation, reading, nature walks, and any other activity that happens. What happens in the free group is that the group tends to come up with the same norms that are listed in Table 2. They decide to talk about the here-and-now, deal with feelings, get personal, respond to each other nonverbally, and avoid past history because they find from group experience that these norms and activities are more growth-producing than alternative ways of working.

The most effective leader for a TORI experience is one who is able to be relatively role free. The next section of this chapter contains a discussion of the behavior of the professional leader in a TORI group. Under many conditions such as those described above the events in a TORI group are well within the range of activities that happen in a group therapy or group sensitivity-training session led by a competent professional therapist or trainer. Under most conditions, the norms and interactions of the group members are prepotent over the leader interventions as determiners of the growth climate of the group. Professionals differ greatly in style. A wide range of behaviors of professionals is apparently effective in training groups. There is little clear evidence on the effects of either group therapy or sensitivity training, so it is difficult to state with any precision the effects of professional style.

The TORI leader comes into the group with several clear intentions. These intentions are described and listed in column two of Table 2. The leader comes in with the intent to be personal, human, open, self-determining, and interdependent. He intends to learn rather than to teach. He intends to respond spontaneously to the moment rather than to program his responses in advance. He feels that he will meet his role responsibilities as a therapist or professional trainer by being as fully a person as it is possible for him to be.

The leader attempts to be relatively free of role, role demands, role obligations, role prescriptions, and role expectations. It is obvious that any consistent pattern of behavior can be called a role, that in retrospect one can call attention to the role that a person is taking. Thus, an observer can say that the person was taking the role of a supporter, an initiator, a parent, or even of a spontaneous person. It is easy to see that in the extreme instance anyone who is following a theory of therapy or training is attempting to program his behavior in advance to respond in particular ways: to reflect feelings, to confront silence, to help members to learn to fight, to reject dependency bids, to focus on conflict resolution, and the like. The TORI leader says that he intends to respond spontaneously to his feelings and perceptions at the moment of response, without consciously censoring or filtering his response in order to be helpful, relevant, supportive, confronting, or effective. It is obvious that no person, whatever his intent or aspiration, can, for example, be completely "free" of response habits, stereotypical responses to people whom he has coded in advance as "paranoidal" or "hostile," "oughts" that keep him from showing anger to people for whom his professional training would prescribe restraint, programmed ways of handling conflict, or conventional or fear-deter-

mined facades. But all persons, no matter how free or spontaneous
or personal, have vestigial elements of conscious role playing. Whenever a person is aware of his own performing, for instance, he is
partially "in role," in the sense we are using the term.

There is no dichotomy between being in role and being personal, but we can point to a clear continuum in theory, and naive
observers can reach agreement in deciding on which of two occasions a person was being "more personal." In TORI theory,
movement toward being personal more of the time is a movement
toward growth. As groups grow and as persons grow there is movement in the directions spelled out in Table 2. Given a free environment of interaction, groups move in these directions. The more the
group moves in these directions the more growth-inductive the
climate, the more persons grow, and the more effective the group.

Members of the group get cues from other members, and in
this sense one person may serve as a "model" for another member.
The TORI leader, however, does not enter the group with the intention of modeling behavior for other members. He comes in with
the intention of learning from others, and learning with others.
Members also tend to repeat behavior that is rewarded. The leader
does not come in with the intention of rewarding effective behavior
and punishing ineffective behavior, and thus teaching effective behavior. The leader expresses genuine feelings and perceptions when
they occur. He expresses warmth toward another person when he
feels warm toward the person. His expression of warmth may be
rewarding, just as any expression of warmth is rewarding to a person who needs warmth. He does not express warmth with the intent
to teach.

The behaviors and foci listed in column two of Table 2
come as a natural flow from this generalized intent to be personal.
As members become less fearful and more trusting they move inevitably toward these behaviors.

Members are impersonal because they are afraid. Inex-
perienced leaders report a number of fears: fear of letting things
get out of hand or losing control; fear that I will be seen as unprofessional and not role worthy; fear that someone for whom I am
responsible will get hurt or have a psychotic episode; fear that I

Table 2
THE PERSONAL OR "ROLE-FREE" RELATIONSHIP

Movement away from:	*Movement toward:*
1. Being "in role"	1. Being "personal"
2. Focus on role-role relations	2. Focus on person-person relations
3. Selecting my behaviors because they are helpful or therapeutic (role prescriptions)	3. Responding to my current feelings and perceptions (showing my self)
4. Responding to what patients or members seem to need (programming)	4. Responding to how I see and feel about our relationships now (being spontaneous)
5. Responding to the other as a patient, client, or "person needing help"	5. Responding to the other as a unique person, *qua* person
6. Screening responses and revealing appropriate, relevant, professional, or role aspects of self	6. Minimal screening, but sharing all areas of self, however relevant or professional
7. Being consistent with a theory of action, therapy, or group growth	7. Focus upon intuition, and "gut feel" of what to do
8. Concern for curing, or remedying the "sick" individual	8. Concern for growth and development of each of us and of our relationships
9. Focus upon motives, interpretations, and other derivative, inferential, or role concepts	9. Focus upon more available, direct, experienced and visible behavior
10. Focus on separate, autonomous individuals or entities, as entities	10. Focus on *relationships* (on how it is now between or among us)
11. Focus on abstraction, generality, principle, or moral judgments	11. Focus on concrete, primitive and elemental feelings and perceptions
12. Focus on and concern for *then* (other relationships in the past, and on the past history of members)	12. Focus on and concern for *now* (how each of us feels and sees things at this moment)
13. Focus on and concern for *there* (data from other relationships and contexts)	13. Focus on and concern for *here* (feelings and perceptions visible and available to all)

will be seen as producing the trauma or the episode; fear that I will not live up to the godlike qualities with which members have endowed me; fear that I will not measure up to other therapists the members have heard about or experienced; fear that I will be seduced or trapped by a member and that I will not know how to respond; fear that I will become personally involved with the members as persons and will thus lose my objectivity and capacity to give appropriate help; fear that members might see other persons in the group as more effective or helpful than I am; and fear that I will not measure up or respond adequately in a crisis when the group looks to me for protection or insight. These and other kindred fears are common to leaders and therapists. They are very much like the fears that all of the other members of the group are having. Each of them is a function of role taking. Only as I see myself as a role do I have these fears. When I come to see myself as a person among other persons these fears dissipate. In a deep and fundamental sense, then, these fears are related to role and serve the function of role maintenance. Each person in the group, including the leader, comes to the point of learning this insight. But each person must learn it many times in many different situations before he comes to *feel* the dysfunctional nature of the role behavior and comes to be more personal.

Perhaps the most significant and central learning in the TORI group is that persons are not frightening or harmful. When I as a person meet another as a person, in deep and meaningful contact, I will not be harmed. When I am a role meeting a role then I can be harmed, the world may be threatening, and my fears are more justified. When a dissenter shows hatred of a bigot it is role responding to role. When a counterdependent member punishes the leader as an authority figure it is role responding to role. When an overtalker finally mobilizes enough anger at a silent person to turn to him in resentment, it is an instance of role punishing role. When persons come to see themselves as persons, show their humanness to others, see the personhood in the others, and establish contact in authenticity and intimacy—then feelings may still be present, angers and hurts may be deep, but the expression of them will be cleansing and productive of further intimacy and contact rather than hurtful and productive of further hurt and distancing. Persons respond less and less to vestigial fathers, enemies, and old girl friends, and more and more to persons who are here, now, and full of feeling. A relationship is responded to for what it is now and not for what it represents or for what use it may be put to. Persons are responded to more for what they are and less for what they seem to be in my projections or in their presenting selves.

The only way that the leader can enter into this person contact and this emerging community of search is to enter as a person. There are many barriers to this entry. Initially, many members will demand a leader. Members, in role as members, will demand protection, wisdom, help, arbitration, therapy, challenge, advice, interpretations, teaching, modeling, rewards, and other leader gifts. They will demand these because these are what they expect as rightful pay for their tuition, fees, or membership. This is what they have come to expect of leaders. They have role obligations that relate to my role demands. The leader will have many internal forces that keep him in role. It is great to be king when one wants to be king and the subjects demand it. Leaders enter into the helping professions because they want to be helpful. The leader may see himself as having special wisdom, unusual skills, strength with which he can protect the weak, a theory that will increase insights, knowledge that will be new and relevant, and effective teaching skills. He may see himself as a professional (a role). One solution to this dilemma is for the professional to see himself as meeting his professional role obligations best by being a person among persons. But the leader has to learn this for himself; it is not something he can be taught.

Fears dissipate with intimate experiences in TORI groups. With interaction in depth over sustained periods of time members inevitably become more open, more direct in communication, more available to others, more human, more interdependent, and more trusting. Members are less frightening as they divest themselves of role and become more personal. Several intense experiences in such groups increase the trust of persons in themselves, in the processes of groups, and in other persons. Leaders come to know that groups will grow and that persons will grow in interaction. Leaders find out for themselves that members will not get hurt, that wisdom is present in all members of the group, that members learn from each other, that warmth and love emerge in the group as members experience each other in depth, that therapeutic events occur as a natural product of depth interaction, that people are not weak and help-needing, that people have unguessed potential for growth and power, that groups and persons can be trusted to grow without special help from leaders-as-roles.

As his trust grows the leader-person can be more helpful. People do grow. The rate of growth can be accelerated. The greater the number of persons who are willing and able to be deeply personal in a given group, the greater the potential for growth in the group. Thus, the leader-as-person can be a powerful influence in the group, just as any other free, powerful, spontaneous, and interdependent person can be a powerful influence for growth.

The TORI leader gets his satisfactions in the group from depth of relationship, from excitement in his own learning, from the rewards of interdependence, from the aesthetic joys of seeing the emergence of a growing group, from the confrontation with personhood, from seeing atrophy and stagnation become zest and movement, and from the growing congruence between his gut and his actions. He gradually becomes emancipated from the transitory and doubtful pleasures of being responsible for others, being worshiped for one's mystical powers, being admired for one's esoteric wisdom, being the protector of the weak, being the good St. Bernard with timely aid in moments of emergency, being a fountain of relevant knowledge, having power over others, being a "real pro," and being granted early deification. The TORI theory is based upon the assumption that the deepest needs of man are to trust and be trusted, to be in intimate communication, to actualize one's inner self, and to be genuinely interdependent. The needs to have power over others, to withdraw to safety, to be worshiped, and to maintain role are real needs, but they are transitory, peripheral, and basically counterdefensive mechanisms which disappear or reduce with defense-reductive experiences over a period of time. Being a role-free group leader is more deeply satisfying to all people over a period of time than is being a more conventional therapist, helper, teacher, or guru.[6]

The group is a continually emerging organism. The five goals of training listed earlier tend to be met as products of inter-action-in-growth. Emergence and growth are products of group interaction. The leader takes no *special* responsibility for the group or member growth, but he does take full responsibility for his own growth and for what happens in the group, just as every other person tends to do as a new awakening comes from caring, commitment, intimacy, and feelings of membership. The leader is not a passive, nondirective, or abdicating member. He enters the action, shares his fears, expresses his preferences for actions and people, gets into trouble, gets angry, falls in love, sits where he feels like sitting, tests his own hypotheses about his own behavior, reveals his humanness, and is present. TORI theory optimizes the opportunity for persons to take full responsibility for their own actions and behavior. When the assigned leader refuses to take responsibility for the group and its goals and clearly communicates in his behavior that each person is free to take responsibility for his own behavior and is free to influence group goals as they emerge, forces are set in motion that optimize individual assertiveness and action.

When the norms listed in Table 2 emerge it is highly likely that during a period of five days of intensive interaction persons will experience their own growth and will have a full experience in a growing group. The critical condition for learning is that individuals have the opportunity under their own initiative to try out new patterns of behavior that they find congruent with emerging new goals, and that they have the opportunity to get clear and caring feedback on this new behavior. It is not necessary that the learner have tension, anxiety, or pain in order to learn. Learning may be a completely exhilarating experience. Insight is not a necessary or sufficient condition for learning. Understanding, sensitivity, and insight may be helpful for learning under certain conditions

---

[6] Gibb, J. R. "The Counselor as a Role-Free Person." In C. A. Parker (Ed.), *Counseling Theories and Counselor Education.* Boston: Houghton Mifflin, 1968.

but do not necessarily lead to new or more effective behavior. The basic and central aspect of the TORI experience is that persons have an opportunity, in a growth climate, to continue to try out new behavior, to experiment with one's own hypotheses about one's life, to live a new life for a time in an environment that is real, supportive, and interdependent. For full and enduring growth that is under the control of the learner it is important that the learner reward himself, that he create conditions that give him the rewards he seeks. There is ample demonstration that people can manipulate the learning of other people by giving them differential rewards and punishments. When someone comes under the power of another's reinforcement schedule (mother's love, teacher's grades or head pats, therapist's encouragement) he is not growing, in the sense that the term is used here.

The TORI group is an environment where experimentation occurs. Persons try out new behavior. Groups plan, create, test, hypothesize, move, feel, and act. New patterns of decision making, organizing, communicating, and relating continually emerge. New forms create themselves. This can be seen to happen with great acceleration when groups restrict verbalization and communicate with touch, smell, movement, sounds, and without words. Emotionality is integrated into the experience. Later, words and theories are integrated into the experience. Full living and growth is an integration of the total organism into continuing emergence of new form and life. Modern man has so truncated his living that it is deprived of the full range of feelings. Modern education builds forces that cause atrophy of feelings and emotions. In full growth thoughts are enriched by feelings and feelings are enriched by thoughts. It is precisely in the full and unprogrammed interplay of the role-free structure that this integration of all facets of life can best occur. The fabric of social control is woven from caring, love, and emergent commitment and interdependence—not from role obligations, responsibilities, and duties.

IV

On $n+1$ Person Groups

Bernard Steinzor

Enthralled by the emergence of what some have called the second psychiatric revolution, and clearly participating in its benefits professionally, we psychotherapists have become provincial in our points of view about our particular place in history. Our comparative security in the established order has, however, recently been challenged by social forces not of our own making. We have found ourselves directly caught up in social currents that force us to the grudging admission that many of our views are less than unique, and are in fact shared by many ordinary citizens who see themselves engaged in the same tasks that we ourselves espouse—the making of a different and better world.

The shock of this realization stems in large part from our own conviction that our perception of reality was the only meaningful one, that the perception of the impelling demands of the inner life and the assumption that the qualities of this inner life could surmount any unfortunate external facts of social life. But we are now called upon to review this conviction, to examine it not as an empirically established truth, but as an ideology, a political position to which we have been committed. This we must do in the face of the now obvious fact that objective social conditions breed their own distress, their own violence and rebellion.

Our conviction of the meaningfulness of the inner man, of his ability and desire to direct his own affairs, has a long and compelling history. It is a part, though indeed only one part, of the American ideology itself—that part which stresses the individuality of the person and his right to self-determination. The unconscious, as a block to this self-determination in individual instances, was known long before Freud. But its discovery by Freud and others assumed a certain neutrality on the part of social and economic conditions. It assumed that the individual, with or without help, but centrally by reconstruction of his own inner convictions, could overcome difficult circumstances. There is evidence enough that this may indeed be true for those persons for whom the objective social and economic conditions are not truly burdensome. But the aim of freely expressing your inner feelings, of developing new ways of communicating with friends and family, assumes a social system in which these end points are truly possible, a social system which, with a little help, permits and encourages these evidences of individuality and self-determination.

But what of those individuals for whom this is not the case, those persons whose real social and economic conditions do not permit this freedom, this option to develop and expand? What of those persons for whom increased intimacy is meaningless—or dangerous? What of those persons whose sense of distress and violence is so intertwined with deplorable social conditions that no rearrangement of the inner life can possibly help?

There may, of course, be some parallels that can help us with a new conception of mental health and with a new group of persons. Personal powerlessness, with which we are familiar in individual psychotherapeutic settings, may have an important parallel in political powerlessness. Increased interpersonal intimacy may still be a crucial value for all peoples, but may well be gained for some through the attained power that comes with the achievement of social and economic justice. Our experiences with groups may stand us in good service if instead of seeing the group in its relation to the inner self we can come to see it in relation to the society at large. We are prepared for the notion that the individual's experiences with the groups around him constitute one of the main influences upon his life, upon his development of a sense of selfhood. The special problem arises, however, when the groups of which many are a part are themselves disenfranchised and impoverished.

A person who is a leader of a group during a period when there is a recognized need for social change has the special opportunity to raise the manifold personal concerns of its members to a level of shared feelings and a common fate. During a time of great social convulsion, such a leader may produce a revolution. A psychotherapist, whether he is with one or more than one person, does just what political leaders do, and if the need for change is based on life and death issues, as with suicidal people or patients in remote wards, revolutionary tactics are more likely to result. What differentiates one system from another are merely disagreements over which contents of the exchange between patient and therapist are believed to make for efficacious change. But from the patient's view, he must experience in one way or another the fact that his anguished private world is a matter of concern to others. I am only reminding us of the obvious: that therapists have formal status and that they must convey somehow that they care. Whatever techniques he uses, the therapist does show the person that he is not the only one who has had the complaints for which he seeks help. He experiences again and again that the doctor does not see him as a unique case at the same time that the doctor's probity is directed toward special differences.

The first advantage claimed for group therapies has been that each member quickly sees that others are also adrift on the same sea. The healing of oneself thus becomes a healing of a community whose members hopefully also can deeply recognize each other as fellow sufferers, and recognize that their meeting is based upon the principle of equal rights among them. Each grants to the others the same rights of expression, confrontation, and negation that he takes for himself.

In situations where one can come and go voluntarily, the achievement of integration and integrity is considerably easier. When, however, people are locked in, and must face the fact of unequal power, then we rightly fear that rage may emerge as physical violence. We can no longer omit from our conceptualizations that power has been always one of the two significant dimensions between the doctor and the patient and between the patient and his significant others.

Belatedly, then, we are coming to the realization that we have been power brokers, intermediaries in a confluence of social conflict, arbitrators between the hard-eyed and the soft-eyed. We had recognized, much earlier, that we were marriage brokers, concerned with questions of intimacy, sexuality, and the achievement of harmony. We have given different labels to the loftiest of dreams, a world of love and harmony, with some calling it intimacy, others calling it interpersonal sensitivity, the art of loving, or the peak experience.

I like the word *intimacy* and I think that what I call intimacy has been within the dominant mood of psychotherapists. I also think that more and more of us believe that a person will enhance his striving for affection if he at the same time seeks for social justice.[1]

I try to separate the person before me from others by monitoring my awareness of his impact on me and then sharing this with him. Gradually, the obvious and usual categories within which the respective frames we put around each other—sex, class, height, attractiveness, temperament, and so forth—give way to an exchange of images neither of us had revealed to anyone else before. The roles, or rather the ways we have learned to modulate and modify the tides of living from birth to our present moments, recede and then give emphasis to the core of ourselves, our relation to the unknown. Then we have met as persons. Our respective social categories only provide the setting for the emergence of whatever our

[1] Steinzor, B. *The Healing Partnership: The Patient as Colleague in Psychotherapy.* New York: Harper, 1967.

special senses and imagination will lead us to in the direction of
compatibility. In striving for intimacy through a critique of the
social systems which have formed our dispositions and our proclivi-
ties for understanding one another, the person and I expose ourselves to the risks of finding ourselves at strenuous odds and con-
cluding that we should separate. I have come to be always ready
to consider a break with another without pejoratives about running
away, flights into health, and the like. The sense of choice is an
existential fact, and thus calls for respecting the person's right to
sever forever our relationship. The increased emphasis on authenticity, congruence with one's feelings, and, also, confrontation are
only a few of the terms reflecting a shift away from the traditional
way of defining contact. This places me in a larger community. I
am not only affirmed by the special pleasures of the intimate exchange, but also by the sense that what I emphasize for the other
is also meant for the future. I see that I am partaking in my
particular way in the development of

> a society in which all the mutual relations of its members are
> regulated by mutual agreements . . . and by a sum of social
> customs and habits, not petrified by law, routine or superstition,
> but continually developing and continually readjusted.[2]

This quotation—from one of the founders of anarchism,
Prince Kropotkin—is, of course, intended to buttress the point that
when we emphasize the values of becoming, we are consonant with
the most radical of political ideals. As many have pointed out,
Freud's method was revolutionary in his emphasis on listening to
all the musings of another. This itself is an unqualified act of love,
which anyone knows when he feels he has been heard. Psychoanalysis, as a concept of the possibilities of relationship, was a
counterforce to the categorization (that is, dehumanization) of men,
which itself fell into its own forms of categorization and defacement
as it became an institution. But that is an old, old irony of historical
fact. The codification of progressive ideas itself brings about a new
bureaucratization which the ideas were intended to abolish. At our
best, then, we are, in our clinical practice, in love with the ideal

[2] Quoted as part of an article by P. Goodman, "The Black Flag of
Anarchism," *New York Times Magazine*, July 14, 1968.

of progress, permanent revolutionaries, suspicious of systems, and open-minded as scientists.

To illustrate this line of argument, let us consider briefly the debate over the relative merits of individual therapy versus group therapy. The very label *individual therapy,* as persistent as it is, was always, and has now come to be recognized explicitly as, a misnomer, in light of reflection on the interpersonal transaction between patient and therapist. We should rather speak of two-or-more-person groups. This can get us beyond the usual arguments, which are merely debates over tactics, tastes, and, of course, economics. Usually, the smaller the group, when led by a certified professional, the higher the cost per member. Any private tutorial requires a considerable personal investment in a society only slowly moving toward the socialization of education, medical costs, and a minimum standard of living. The substantive issues, in the sense that we think we have something directly to say about them, are the contents of our talks with others, the recognitions we give to nonprofessional efforts at healing, and the conception we have of the nature of the self. These are closely related issues; they have been argued in the literature most vigorously in the debates over the medical model and the interpretation of the studies on outcome of the various methods of therapy.

The three-or-more-person groups, whether we call such gatherings marathons, Esalens, Synanons, sensitivity training, or whatever, are in part signs of an emerging challenge to the traditional view that intimacy can grow only in a private relationship between two persons. They are all manifestations of the values of love dispersed into ever-widening circles. They provide possibilities for warmth and intimacy in a culture where friendship provides little comfort. We should thus welcome the spread of various kinds and sizes of groups. The more there are, the more possible it becomes for a person to find a setting which will be more beneficial than harmful. The spread of techniques and the multiplication of systems and settings are not, as some have said, a reflection of chaos but rather the elaboration of equity and intimacy thought by us to be possible only in the two-person group.

Many patients and therapists prefer to be in groups larger

than two persons because they believe they get on faster and better this way. Faster and better than what and for whom? Can any expert be anything but modest in recommending one form of therapy over another? We should remember Alcoholics Anonymous, perhaps the original group in which nonprofessional leadership was shown to be superior to professional therapists for the relief of a socially recognized malady. This setting did work for those who found themselves welcomed. And that should be our model: the encouragement of persons to shop around, to open their sensibilities toward the possibilities of various groups, natural and organized, as offering therapeutic possibilities.

I do think that the common goal of our n+1 person therapies, namely self-revelation (this applies as well to so-called behavior therapies, because the therapist establishes a context for operant conditioning) must be given its greatest test eventually in the two-person group. Or perhaps in the way the person acts in the larger community. Or better still, the way the person becomes a freer citizen and a freer lover. Or as one theologian put it: "In God, justice and love are ultimately one. Therefore, in principle the command to love is also a command to seek justice."[8]

I wish to make this point in another way. The more I have found my way and realized that I always do what I am, the more I have felt the thought control implicit in the concept of acting-out. The dichotomy between thought and action requires reconceptualization in view of recent social movements. In my own experience, the people who grant me the opportunity to work with them need to be encouraged to act in the world, as well as to get in touch with their dreams, feelings, and fantasies. I have come to the belief that our therapies (and again I am including behavior modification therapy) tend to push the person toward self-centered absorption. Do the behavior modification people ever investigate phobias which other people call ethnic prejudice? Perusal of case reports involving the various techniques suggests that the patient is only muddled about those persons called mother, father, lover, wife, husband, or boss, and never about political persons whose actions have at least

[8] Williams, D. D. *What Present-Day Theologians Are Thinking.* New York: Harper, 1967, p. 130.

as much to do with his general welfare as those he is encouraged to discuss. The vital political and social issues of the day are hardly given attention in the public records of therapeutic transactions. It is as if we reduce a conflict about politics to the same level as chit-chat about the weather. The family of man begins and ends with one's own family. The consulting room becomes an inner sanctum. For the purpose of summarizing the views in this polemic on our social values as therapists, I will trichotomize our various allegiances into the classicists, the centrists, and the avant-gardists.

The Classicists: The members of this caucus are largely found in training institutions, pre- and postdoctoral. These leaders of the establishment have faith in progress when it is grounded in the development of basic knowledge leading to general laws. Issues, they say, are always complex and only through reasonable exchange, good will, and patient compromise can they be clarified. This must also be done under the guidance of a formally trained expert properly certified. The levels of formal training are qualifications for levels of functioning and responsibility. The more the formal training the more the practitioner or scientist is presumed to be able to discriminate between questions of fact and questions of value. Consensus and compromise are prime values since they are more likely to produce orderly change, and transformation of laws through established procedures are the only ways that produce enduring transformations. A revolution is suspect since history reveals that extremes always produce their opposites. Violence of any kind is assumed to be counterproductive.

Individual responsibility for one's own demonic forces must be primarily manifested in a continuous and large expenditure of effort to master one's inner life. When assailed by critics about the need for reformation of social systems, the classicist agrees but then adds the strong qualification that, in the final analysis, the only sustaining philosophy is the effort to find the meaning of the human condition. The attitude of enduring life as tragic does occasionally slip into despair, but this is called facing reality. The orthodox psychoanalyst and the modern existentialist both subscribe to the felt experience expressed by Boris Pasternak: "To live life to the end is not a childish task."

The Centrists: Making one's way, or making it, requires an astute combination of adjustments to the structure of endowed-with-power institutions, and just enough originality to attract a following. You keep up with the times, which means today an increasing support of the submerged voices, which have been around for years, but now seize our attention because of circumstances beyond our control. Being a centrist means that you do dissent from some of the valued actions of your reference group, but you certainly do not challenge the institution.

It is quite evident that many recent studies of the efficacy of treatment lead to the simple conclusion that the relatively untrained person does as well and sometimes better than we who have knocked around in the academic halls and training institute corridors for some of the best years of our lives. In scientific candor, we duly print the reports of these studies. But I have yet to hear of any regular institution changing its recruitment policy. Though some curriculum changes do occur, with courses on community psychiatry and psychology most favored, the professors are adequately degreed. Some candid union leader might tell us better what not to do than those of us who have had our organizing experience in such settings as child guidance clinics and public schools.

Thus the centrist appears to have the best of both worlds: he is anchored in research and the primacy of the intellect but also open to the clamor of the new politics. Abandoning the medical model and adopting an educational one is now a fashionable move. The centrist is a scientific humanist and gradually, through his accumulated wisdom, underscores the humanistic view that a man's character unfolds in a social network. The questions that need research are socially relevant ones, and they turn to social psychologists, for example, to testify that children as well as rats learn better when encouraged and expected to do so. If he is caught up in an immediate community issue, the centrist is likely to become radicalized. Once he allows that functioning is more significant than entitlements, then polarization as well as fellow feeling develops. The centrist in a rapidly developing situation feels renewed because his involvement with the treatment of groups brings him new experiences and new life.[4]

The Avant-Gardists: This approach gives emphasis to the value the community places on a man's public work. A man's actual occupation and the dignity it affords, as well as its money value, are what determines his identity. Thus any theory of sublimation is seen as a diversion from the actualities of a person's experience in the economic and social order. The avant-gardist conceives of human nature as unfolding and changing through the conditions of existence. Equity of power, economic and social, must be achieved as the foundation for private love and harmony. Inequity is the cause of rage, and the grosser the injustice, the greater the violence. The erosion of established authority is welcomed and the proof of the avant-gardist's faith is seen in the disobedience of Catholics, in student demonstrations, and in all voices which equate revolution with free imagination, spontaneity, participation, and communion.

Action with others is valued as the process through which one achieves understanding of one's feelings. It is anticipated that a fringe of violence will often accompany social and personal change. An almost unexceptional law, for this kind of person, is that no one, including therapists, shares power and privilege without being provoked and pushed to doing so. People must scream before they are appreciated and can love. The favored tactic in the consultation room as well as in the streets is direct encounter and confrontation in order to break up the roles we play. Momentary defeats are expected—one takes a step back to take two steps forward.

In the emphasis on dramatization of issues and self-expression, the avant-gardist appears to be anti-intellectual. He sharply questions the need for research, claiming that there is not only enough evidence already lying around in journals and books, but that simple felt experience shows the effects of repression. The avant-gardist speaks with impatience and appears anarchic in his activism. His visions are often utopian, and he requires that contact

[4] See Hentoff, N. *A Doctor Among the Addicts.* New York: Rand McNally, 1968. This is an account of the work of Marie Nyswander.

and "telling it like it is" must be instantly available to everyone. He appears to ride over the way a person's character affects the implementation of his ideologies. The avant-gardist forgets that the qualities that make for adequate leadership at a time of crisis are often the very qualities which are not helpful in the consolidation of gains. At the best he is surprised when his own managerial tendencies are opposed by others, and at the worst he becomes disillusioned with the possibility of progress. At such moments, the avant-gardist may become aware of the coerciveness of basic encounter groups and the like. Honesty may then be seen as a game people play. In one measure or another, we all believe in progress toward a world of love and justice.

V

Encounter—The Game of No Game

Hobart F. Thomas

After sitting quietly alone for a time, it came to me: encounter is meeting reality face to face. It is unbelievably complex; it is miraculously simple. My reality is my experience in the ever-present now.

I am seated in front of a group of students in a college classroom. "Is it possible to deal with some things that really matter to us?" I ask. We will be together for only an hour and fifteen minutes since I am substituting for a colleague who is ill. "Let me hear what you are most interested in right at this minute. What you can put into words I shall write on the board." A young man asks, "How can we break down the barriers between people?" A young woman chimes in, "How do we communicate better with each other?" There is a long pause. No one else responds. I ask myself, "What now?" Shall we talk about the topic of communication? No, let's act instead. "Are you game to experiment a bit?" I ask. There are a few tentative nods from some of the students. "O.K., push the chairs aside, mill around the room and pick out a person you don't know but would like to know better. This may sound a little crazy, but sit on the floor back to back with your partner and carry on a conversation for a few minutes." After a short period of time I ask the pairs to turn around face to face and share their feelings. Next, the pairs face each other and each person takes a turn at mirroring the actions of his partner. We then form groups of eight and share our experiences. After the period of sharing, each member of the group in turn is asked to close his eyes and allow himself to be passed around by the other members, who are standing in a circle. People are now experiencing how much they are willing to let go and trust others to support them. Soon the entire group is standing in a large circle with arms entwined and people are looking at and experiencing each other in a very different way than they were at the beginning of the session. Several express surprise at how much closer they feel to others in the group. During that hour and fifteen minutes, in a very real sense, we dealt with the initial questions of the students regarding interpersonal barriers.

A university counseling center staff of about fifteen has invited me to spend the day with them in a sensitivity-training session. The stated purpose is to deal with interpersonal problems in the hope of improving staff effectiveness. This is a relatively sophisticated group with a variety of experiences in individual and group therapy, sensitivity training, sensory awareness and related activities. Seemingly little of significance has happened throughout the day as the group struggles for authenticity. With little more than an hour remaining I reveal my own feelings of frustration to the group and ask, "What does one do at times like these?" I feel as though I have nothing to offer. An attractive young woman turns to me, eyes flashing in anger, "Well, if *you* don't know, then who does? I had heard a lot about you, and I'm really disappointed. I came here expecting you to turn us on, and you haven't done a damn thing!

Where's your act?" I can only reply, "This *is* my act." I have no suggestions to make, I can only be what I am. Soon she begins to weep and, looking at me and then at her supervisor, with whom she had had great difficulty relating, she exclaims with intense emotion, "Now I really understand. You are people, too! Here I've had you up on high pedestals, fearing you, both admiring and hating you, but I couldn't get close to you. I also expected you to have the answers for me." Looking at others in the room she exclaims, "My God, we're all just human beings and that's great!" This seems to produce an electrifying effect on the group which is no longer stuck on dead center. Persons are communicating with persons rather than roles talking to other roles.

Several years ago I met for a day with a group of about fifteen school administrators in a large eastern city. I began by stating that as far as I was concerned we were free to use this time in any way we wished. It was my hope that all of us could gain the maximum benefit from our session together. Since I sensed a variety of needs and expectations within the group, I remarked that it would probably be a good idea if the members would express these thoughts and feelings as soon as possible. I also made a statement, half in jest, to the effect that even if nothing terribly significant happened, at least all of them could have a day's vacation from work.

Prior to my arrival, some of the participants in the group had heard that encounter groups consisted primarily of hostile exchanges between people. Fairly soon after the group began to meet, a number of people began talking about hostility in various superficial ways. My feeling, which I shared with the group, was that we were like school children going through the motions of what teacher expected of us. I perceived no genuine interest in the topic. I believe I was able to convey to this group, after a period of time, that I was not interested in playing the game of teacher and pupils. I did not think they were, either; but I was most deeply interested in their real concerns even though I was unaware of what they might be. My main interest was that all of us as a group might deal with whatever was most real and vital to us at that moment in time.

As I recall, the morning was not terribly exciting. A good

deal of time was spent getting acquainted in various ways, sharing work experiences and other past events. Some of the group had lunch together, and after we returned, I asked people to write on sheets of paper, without signing their names, the feelings and experiences they were having at that time which they found most difficult to express to others in the group. After I gave a brief talk about some of the theoretical aspects of encounter groups, the papers were read aloud to those present. As I recall, some deeper and particularly more negative feelings about lack of progress in the group thus far were expressed in the written statements.

I cannot remember just how it came about, but all of a sudden a number of people began discussing some very immediate dissatisfactions about their work situations. They were concerned about such matters as poor communication, inadequate representation on school board meetings, lack of group cohesion, and little personal understanding of each other. The group took on a new vitality as they began to discuss the immediate concerns they had in common. They also took specific steps to attempt to remedy the situation by forming their own ongoing group to continue working on these problems.

I had not the slightest idea at the outset that the group would move in this direction. It did seem to me, however, that there was a "rightness" about the way this group moved. Even though I had no direct connection with these problems, had never seen these people before, and have not seen them since, I found this a very alive, meaningful experience for me.

For some time I have struggled with the problem of communicating what for me is the essence of encounter. Hopefully, my attempts to clarify and reflect upon my own experiences may assist you to do likewise for yourself. Earlier I defined encounter as meeting reality face to face. Obviously this includes far more than the phenomenon of encounter groups.

Of primary importance to me is what I would characterize as an attitude of allowing or letting be. I believe this attitude can be cultivated by attending to one's experience at any point in time. It is asking oneself the question "What is?" rather than "What ought to be?" Applied to the individual alone it may consist of attending to such basics as one's bodily sensations—breathing, heartbeat, or various tensions within the body.

Let me share with you some of my present experiences. Perhaps this will serve to illustrate further the meanings I hope to communicate. As I write I experience a conflict. One part of me, so it seems, is attempting to write an orderly, coherent, precise account —something that will be acceptable and approved by an unknown audience. The other part of me seems to want to ramble and play with ideas. The former appears to represent my "shoulds," doing what is expected of me; the latter a looser, perhaps more creative part of myself. Before I focused on these two opposing forces I sat immobilized for many minutes. I finally decided what I wanted to do and acted by describing the experience to you. My action, whatever it is, becomes a synthesis of opposing tendencies. I like to refer to this process as "tuning in on oneself." It is merely paying attention to what I experience at any given moment and asking myself what I want to do. Ruth Cohn, in an intriguing article entitled "I Must Do What I Want to Do: A Therapeutic Game for Therapists, Patients and Other People,"[1] asks the person to do what he wants to do for ten minutes. He is asked to check at every moment whether he is *really* doing what he wants and if not to change and do what he wants to. She makes the important distinction between impulse (what one feels like doing), judgment, and what one *wants* to do by the following illustration: "I might have a fantasy that I want to dance, but my body may signal that I am tired now and what I really want to do is to have a fantasy of dancing. The opposite may be true; I might think dancing is silly but my body may want to dance. I then have to make a decision; which is what I want? And the decision may come effortlessly by itself, within a few seconds, or a third idea may pop up and ring the bell of 'this is it!' "

As I view it, this tuning in on oneself and doing as one wants to do is one of the most important things I know. Yet, how easy it is to get out of touch. Recently I have paid more attention to this process of tuning in by asking people in groups I conduct to spend a period of time in silence just to find out where they are before interacting with each other. For any of us in a group, the process

[1] Cohn, R. C. "I Must Do What I Want To," *Voices, 4,* 1968.

of tuning in is further complicated by the variety of needs, expectations, and overt behavior of other people. I have found that the
most meaningful group experiences seem to occur when people (1)
are aware of what is going on in themselves, (2) listen attentively
and empathically to others, and (3) share their experiences, thoughts,
and perceptions with each other. This all sounds so simple yet it
often seems difficult in practice. It is anything but easy for people to
listen attentively to each other or, on the other hand, to express their
real feelings before they have spent considerable time together. A
human being has many facets. Their external mannerisms and defenses often act as mutual irritants. People are like porcupines with
sharp quills who repel each other as they try, in their own fumbling
ways, to get close. They attack and defend, they soliloquize or remain silently in a shell, they vie with each other for attention or
control. They may endure hellish periods of anguish and despair as
they face insoluble problems.

Often, as a group facilitator, I find that my own feelings
are very closely related to those of others in the group. It is not
always easy to tell whether my suffering is primarily related to my
own private world or a reflection of the suffering of others. Whatever the case, going through the dark night of the soul is very much
a part of the group experience. Many, many times when involved
in the deep negative aspects of the encounter group I have seriously
questioned whether anything could be worth this much suffering.
If one proposes to meet or encounter what actually exists in human
experience then indeed one must be willing to suffer. I do not have
to look for it; it is just there.

It appears to me that much of my day-to-day existence lacks
the intensity of the encounter group experience. It is quite possible
that most human beings would find it difficult, if not impossible, to
maintain such a level of intensity. Also, in the encounter group, the
peaks and valleys of experience are compressed into a relatively
brief time. Whatever the case, the encounter group appears to be
a microcosm of experience which offers the person a glimpse of what
is possible in the human venture.

Time and again I have found that if one is willing to see it
through, the encounter group experience is well worth the trip.

Most significant to me is the fact that most of those who commit themselves to the venture in a relatively brief span of time are able to experience highly rewarding states of being. Being is of value in itself. People are able to accept themselves and each other just as they are. Deep, genuine caring for others occurs, and people know what it means to love. Some of these experiences are so profound that they can be described as transcendental or religious.[2]

I have found, however, that the more I look for the great enlightenment, the less likely I am to find it. My most significant experiences have occurred at times when I least expected them. Oftentimes they have been preceded by and seem to stem from periods of suffering and despair. As far as I can recall, they never are associated with the times I try to make things happen.

Again, I must come back to what is for me the essential attitude of attending—allowing, letting be. Closely allied with this is a trust in the nature of things. How often I fall short of this trust. Even though in the past each dark night of despair has been followed by a dawn of joy, there is no guarantee that it will be true this time. Yet, life is change, and that which I experience as me is a constant process of change. To what extent can I allow myself to trust and flow with this process? Is it possible for me to be sensitively aware of me, my realm of experience in the moment? How difficult also to allow other people to really see me as I am. Not too long ago I was acting as a consultant for a group of people all of whom were active as group leaders. I suddenly found myself unconsciously sucked into the role of playing expert. What I was doing seemed wrong for me. I became obviously anxious and fumbling in my answers. I shared with the group some of my feelings at that moment which had to do with how little I felt like a leader then. I was frightened because I did not know whether I really dared to reveal my true feelings. I was being anything but a leader in the conventional sense; however, without consciously intending to do so, I was demonstrating what I consider most important—namely, the willingness to face where one is and to share it with others.

[2] Clark, J. V. "Toward a Theory and Practice of Religious Experiencing." In J. F. T. Bugental (Ed.) *Challenges of Humanistic Psychology.* New York: McGraw-Hill, 1967.

Interestingly enough, several persons, including myself, at that point became acutely aware of the importance of seeking the answer within rather than looking to the expert. The tone of the meeting changed to one of sharing feelings and searching together for answers.

In my opinion, the most essential task for the group facilitator is that of developing the courage to be and allowing himself to be known by others. So often at any given point in time what I am is in conflict with what I think I ought to be or what others expect from me. I may feel devoid of knowledge and wisdom in situations where I am considered to be the expert, such as the illustration given above. I may feel playful when others are serious or vice versa. I may feel completely out of harmony with the conventional rules of the game, which just about everybody else seems to be taking for granted. For the most part, I believe my effectiveness is directly related to my ability to accept myself and allow others to see me as I am. Essentially this involves a conscious recognition of my immediate experience and a willingness to share it openly with others.

Some of my most frustrating experiences as a group facilitator have occurred at times when I tried to be like someone else. My attempts to adopt the techniques of people whom I admire usually fall far short of what I would consider success experience for anyone. If, on the other hand, I am able to pay close attention to what feels right to me and risk being myself, I have found that this, in turn, allows others to accept and be themselves.

Given the right environment, the process of growth appears to happen spontaneously of its own accord. Often I succumb to the desire to be the great leader who somehow makes it happen. Yet, in the final analysis, I can be at best a type of psychological midwife who aids and abets that which is about to be born. One might well raise the question, "Are there psychological gestation periods analogous in any way to the physical?" Although I am genuinely impressed by recently developed techniques[3] which bring about almost immediate involvement and intimacy between people at what appear to be deep levels, I am very much concerned with the problem of how each person develops his own sense of autonomy

[3] Schutz, W. C. *Joy*. New York: Grove Press, 1967.

in ways that are right for him. How much struggle must he endure of his own? Are there shortcuts to personal growth? I value most highly the goal of each person's finding answers within himself rather than looking outward to a great leader for the answers. It seems very important that I, as a group facilitator, do not lose sight of this basic goal. To me, the encounter group is essentially an experiment with freedom. I believe we are putting to the test the assumption that in a climate where people are free to be whatever they are, they will move in growth-enhancing directions. We are also testing the assumption that at his deepest levels the individual is capable of knowing what is right for him. Thus far, in my experience, these assumptions have been supported. Interestingly enough, the concept of the self-fulfilling prophecy seems relevant. I am convinced that the attitude of the facilitator has a very profound influence. If he trusts, people tend to be trustworthy. If he mistrusts and for whatever reasons manipulates, people tend to become distracted from the quest of finding their own sources of inner direction.

As I write this I ask myself how one develops this trust in the nature of things. My own sense of trust falters on many occasions. I recall instances of violent hatred when people seemed to be tearing each other apart. Then there are the periods of utter despair as we face what appear to be hopeless problems which defy any solution. There are periods of confusion and frustration at the lack of any meaningful direction. And perhaps most trying of all are the dead phases of sheer boredom which lack even a spark of vitality. Encounter, to me, is the willingness to face all of these experiences, which are part of the human condition. Yes, I must face even the worst of all when it happens—my own lack of trust.

Often, after we have struggled for long periods of time and faced some of the most dismal aspects of reality, something very much akin to the miraculous occurs. I find this difficult to describe precisely. Words such as *pure being, joy, appreciation of the now* come to mind. At times like this I do not ask what this experience is good for. It is of value in itself. People who formerly appeared ugly and commonplace are now, with all of their imperfections, indeed beautiful. I am reminded of a woman who remarked after such an experience, "I would have gladly given my life for any person in that room." Under such circumstances people more often than not experience what it means to deeply love both themselves and others.

The fact that we have the knowledge of how to bring about such relationships between people is, to me, highly significant. I find it puzzling and discouraging at times when I see how apparently minimal has been our progress in implementing such knowledge in our society as a whole. On the other hand, I take heart in the fact that Victor Frankl[4] and others could find meaning to their lives amid the horror of a concentration camp.

Encounter, as I view it, definitely involves facing the experience which life presents to me. At times I appear to have a choice either of meeting or avoiding this encounter. I also strongly suspect that in a very real sense I am a co-creator of this experience. It seems as though I have the choice if I care to exercise it, of moving in directions which are primarily self-enhancing. In general, my self-enhancement seems to include the growth of others about me, so that in taking care of myself I am also most likely to do well by them.

In a very real sense, each encounter group is a happening, a human adventure, a voyage, the destination of which defies determination. It is a subtle interplay of many forces, conscious and otherwise. I find it very similar to my experience in painting. True, at times one takes conscious purposeful action, but one must also allow the picture to paint itself. This requires the willingness to trust and allow the emergence of the seemingly irrational forces which do not neatly fit into preconceived molds. It is a letting go of the conventional and the familiar so that the new may come into being.

I am very much in accord with those who view the encounter group leader as a facilitator rather than one who directs and tells people what to do. As I see it, his main responsibility lies in his ability to allow for the maximum possible development of the forces lying fallow within the group. There is immense potential for healing relationships between people, and I feel that in a climate such as the one I am attempting to describe, that people

[4] Frankl, V. E. *The Doctor and the Soul.* New York: Knopf, 1962.

manifest a natural tendency to seek out others who meet their needs at the moment. This is indeed a type of therapeutic community.

In order for growth to occur, I see the need of two basic factors: nurturance and challenge. I have described these in another paper.[5] Nurturance refers to the acceptance of the person just as he is. I consider it to be very similar to what is meant by unconditional mother love. The child is loved just because he is—not for what he does. As the child grows and develops, however, he soon discovers that much of his behavior is not acceptable to others. He is challenged by both his peers and adults, including parents, who are not about to accept him just as he is at all times. And so, much, if not most, of life consists of the struggle of organisms with each other for survival. If the person is fortunate, he develops and grows strong as a result of pitting himself against obstacles.

I consider one of the important functions of the group facilitator to be that of allowing expression of the two forces of nurturance and challenge. As a facilitator one can only rely on one's feelings as to what is right at any given moment. On some occasions I find myself expressing support (nurturance) for a person; on others, I challenge by expressing irritation or indignation at the responses of people in the group. I value very highly the genuine, open, spontaneous responses whatever they may be.

Without the attitude of nurturance it seems unlikely that the person will develop sufficient strength and self-confidence to meet the challenges of the world. I suspect that such a lack may result either in the overly timid person on the one hand or the extremely defiant, hostile individual on the other. Without adequate challenge, I would suspect a lack of strength and character development to be a real possibility. Without challenge in the group, things tend to go dead and people do not have the opportunity to experience awareness of their defenses and games as viewed by others. Ideally, the functions of nurturing and challenging can be shared by all members of the group.

For some time I have been intrigued with the concept of play. Unfortunately, *play* is a rather ambiguous word. To many it

[5] Thomas, H. F. "The Encounter Group and Some of Its Implications for Education and Life." Rohnert Park, Calif.: Sonoma State College, 1966 (mimeo.).

refers to trivial, unimportant, nonessential behavior. *Play*, as I use
it, represents to me the highest value. It is purposeless behavior but
purposeless only in that it is of value in and of itself. It is not good
for something. Children, totally involved in the ecstasy of the dance,
do not bother themselves with the question "Of what value is this?"
So I would ask myself and you, "Can you find what you enjoy
doing most—just for its own sake—and do it?" If not, why not? I
remember at a weekend workshop shocking one very serious group
member who asked why I was there by replying, "To have a ball."
Unfortunately such remarks are usually misinterpreted and one cannot will a Dionysian festival into being if people are not ready for it.
Often the members of a given group are in different places at the
same time. Harmony can only occur by facing the disharmony and
recognizing it as a part of reality. I know of no alternative but to
face reality as it is and then allow things to happen. As a group
spends time together and people deal with their conflicting needs,
more often than not, a real feeling of harmony eventually emerges.
This can be very deep, embuing almost any event with an aura of
sanctity. One can only find this meaning by going through the
experience himself. Often it involves the most painful of struggles
to arrive there. I know that there are many ways to experience this
deep meaning of life. The encounter group is one. For me it offers
a medium, a springboard which enables me to experience more on
my own. I know of other people who seem to begin alone and rely
far less on groups. Whatever the case, each must find his own way.

I once defined an encounter group as a group of individuals
committed to the task of becoming more fully human. There are no
"have to's." To me, it is a come-and-be-as-you are situation. There
is nothing we *have* to do. I hope we all can learn to do what we
most deeply *want* to do. There is no game we are expected to play.
There are no rules I can think of. It might be helpful to keep in
mind, however, that sticks and stones and not words can indeed
break bones.

In the deepest sense, this, to me, is the goal of the encounter
group and indeed of life itself—to play, to swing, to be in harmony
with self, others, and the universe. The grand game is no game.

VI

A Stage for Trust

Frederick H. Stoller

A group experience can, like sex, encompass a rich complex of emotions: exhilaration, despair, fear, laughter and joy, pain and sorrow. The enriching experience, in and of itself, may be sufficient reason for participation as far as the individual is concerned. But, to take an obvious example, it is the implications beyond the sexual act which account for the continuing flood of speculation and discussion about sex. In much the same way, the implications of the encounter experience, its potential for creating ripples within the individual's life and upon our social styles, are the primary source of interest for the field.

Singer has suggested that one of the possible definitions of well-being could be self-actualization "or the realization of a human being's unique and individual potentialities and the employment of

81

his energies in accordance with his individuality."[1] Growth and
change, new behavioral directions, the realization of potential,
heightened self-awareness, and a richer perception of one's circumstances as well as the circumstances of others are some of the goals
toward which the encounter group strives. While this bears considerable resemblance to psychotherapeutic goals, the assumptions
and procedures arise out of a somewhat different framework and
should be specified as clearly as possible.

Inherent in the clinical approach and in the field of psychotherapy, which is so closely connected with it, is the concept of
psychopathology as a basic explanation for the dysfunctional behaviors of man. It is not necessary to challenge the validity of the
clinical model, merely its exclusivity; alternative views of man
emerge when different populations are involved. People come to
encounter groups not necessarily because they are in difficulty in
their life circumstances (though some are), but because they are
interested in growth despite their state of relative well-being. They
are saying, in effect, "I am doing all right—but there must be more
in myself and in life than I have heretofore experienced." The
motives of such people range from curiosity about themselves to a
hunger for change which reflects shifting forces within them. It is
inevitable, perhaps, that emerging out of such a groundwork a
different image of man becomes explicit.[2]

Built into this alternative view of man are a number of assumptions:

1. At any given moment the human adult possesses a complex variety of possibilities which are often latent but available to
him under the appropriate conditions. The repertoire can be considered a response hierarchy in which certain elements tend to rise
to the level of awareness and action relatively frequently while the
remainder tend to be latent. However, such potential response patterns are available to the individual even though they are infre-

---

[1] Singer, E. *Key Concepts in Psychotherapy.* New York: Random
House, 1965, p. 15.
[2] A somewhat different though much more detailed comparison
between the therapeutic and growth approaches can be found in Durkin, H.
E. *The Group in Depth.* New York: International Universities Press, 1964.

quently enough experienced to remain outside the realm of awareness. New patterns, then, do not necessarily involve completely new
learning sequences but merely the opportunity for latent responses
to emerge.

2. People invest energy in one aspect of themselves at the
expense of others so that one facet of the individual often becomes
much more fully explored and familiar than others. Thus, not only
are there latent response hierarchies which could be available but
there are also familiar and unfamiliar components. These unex-
plored territories include combinations of response patterns, emotional ranges, new cognitive and perceptual integrations, role mix-
tures, suppressed areas of concern among other possibilities. An
extremely important segment of the fallow area consists of talents
which are largely unexercised. Two important considerations concerned with the maintenance of the status quo are: (a) talents and
capacities which are unutilized tend to create and perpetuate conditions of minor but chronic discomfort and uneasiness which
emerge in the form of dissatisfaction, boredom, restlessness, or
melancholy. It is not easy for the person to specify why he feels the
way he does but such states can color and flavor an individual's
life; (b) energy is invested in *withholding* from action and participation and even though muted when compared with the energy that
goes into involvement, there is a cumulative and unceasing expenditure when caution and control are dominant themes. Since,
for most people, the investment in holding back and watching oneself is so ubiquitous, its cost is difficult to evaluate until the pattern
of cautious control has been altered.

3. Latent responses within the hierarchy are often available
and can emerge when the more frequently emitted responses cease
to occur with regularity. Therefore, it is frequently necessary to
stop one set of acts before another set can become evident. Without
negating the presence of long-standing and recalcitrant neurotic
processes within every individual, there are also patterns which are
merely habitual and no longer as necessary as they once were. Stopping such behavior often requires the heightened awareness of their
presence and, with this self-consciousness, a slowing down and halt-

ing of what has heretofore been unreflective conduct. The emergence of alternative responses does not necessarily require lengthy retraining, as is frequently considered the case.

4. Bravery is a necessary quality of every explorer of unknown lands. Similarly, risk-taking is an inherent part of self-exploration. Attempting to delve into that area of the self which has been neglected requires the facing of the unaccustomed and the potentially dangerous. Risk-taking involves a sense of trust, both in oneself and in the world. This sense of trust requires development, investigation, and testing. Nevertheless, too much safety cannot be guaranteed; growth is almost synonymous with risk-taking.

5. Dulled perception about one's course in the world is probably the rule rather than the exception. Falling into routinized and ritualized patterns of life seems to be a natural format; it can be a highly efficient way to operate for a good portion of our lives. It could be an intolerable burden to have to consider goals and purposes every time we get up in the morning. We are thus saved from experiencing pain and anguish as a daily occurrence. But this very capacity for soothing the course of our lives makes it extraordinarily difficult for us to evaluate and reevaluate our stance and direction. Providing that growth and movement are not seen as arising *exclusively* out of crisis, there exists the requirement for periodic opportunities to evaluate where one is and where one is going, to resharpen one's perception of self and of others. Growth is not perceived as a continuous process but rather as functioning in slopes and plateaus. Within this framework, dissatisfaction and unrest are not seen as the inevitable concomitants of life but as possible signals concerning the need for new vistas and reevaluations.

The model for growth and change which has been sketched pertains, seemingly, to the normal adult functioning reasonably adequately.[3] This, or some other analogous model not arising out of exclusively pathological considerations, has been found necessary for groups which operate from a base other than the clinical. It is

[3] Features of this model have been discussed in greater detail in Stoller, F. H. "A Synergic Model for Human Growth." Paper presented in the American Psychological Association Convention, San Francisco, 1968.

now appropriate to consider dimensions of the group which seem most applicable.

Before specifying the frame of reference for the group encounter, I should make it clear that my conception of group encounter is heavily influenced by my experience with marathon groups as specified by Bach[4] and my own writings.[5] In addition, explorations in the utilization of video tape feedback[6] have also colored the following description. Despite such apparent influences, what follows is not designed to be specific to any particular format such as the marathon or the inclusion of video tape but rather to be generally applicable to the basic encounter group, to employ the term used by Rogers.[7]

The encounter group is a place to which people come to learn about themselves for a wide variety of reasons but without any implications that they are in difficulty. The learnings take place through the reactions and reflections of the various group members, through what a participant sees clarified in other participants, and through the relationships and crises that occur both to himself and to others. In this light, the group is a setting in which people come together to rub up against one another so that they may experience others and, ultimately, themselves, more fully.

It is meaningful to look at the dictionary meaning of *encounter:* a meeting with a person or thing, especially when casual or unexpected (a second meaning refers to a hostile meeting, battle, or contest). Although the second meaning characterizes an important portion of the encounter group experience, the first meaning requires primary consideration. In particular, the casual or unexpected nature of the meeting is what is essential to the goals

[4] Bach, G. R. "The Marathon Group: Intensive Practice of Intimate Interaction," *Psychological Reports,* 1966, *18,* 995–1002.

[5] Stoller, F. H. "Marathon Group Therapy." In G. M. Gazda (Ed.) *Innovations to Group Psychotherapy.* Springfield, Ill.: Thomas, 1968.

[6] Stoller, F. H. "Focused Feedback with Video Tape: Extending the Group's Functions." In G. M. Gazda (Ed.) *Innovations to Group Psychotherapy.* Springfield, Ill.: Thomas, 1968.

[7] Rogers, C. R. "The Process of the Basic Encounter Group." In J. F. T. Bugental (Ed.) *Challenges of Humanistic Psychology.* New York: McGraw-Hill, 1967.

of the group. Translated into interaction terms, this means unprogrammed and spontaneous contact—a coming together without
the necessity for maneuver, filtering, or distortion; it means allowing
various levels of the person to be known as freely as possible. For
the opposite of encounter, we can look at some of the definitions
of *counter:* to give a blow while receiving or parrying one; to make
a countermove. Within the context of interaction, countering can
be seen as handling or dealing with, rather than making contact.
Internal restructuring on the part of one of the recipients of an
interaction cannot occur simultaneously with listening and considering.

An important goal of the group is to help participants move
through and beyond their countering efforts toward the encounter
with others. In this way they come to know the world, or some important sample of that world, as it really exists rather than as their
fantasies or preconceptions continuously redefine it. But the ultimate
goal is the individual's encounter with himself. As the dialogue
extends from the person to the others, so it extends within himself.
It is assumed that the group member's dealings with others only
reflect his dealings with himself. If he cannot state his own motives
and goals clearly to others, he cannot state them clearly to himself.
If he floods with explanations and boredom as a way of exhausting
others, he sets up a similar cloud within himself. Encountering oneself, developing a dialogue which clarifies and specifies what one
is about, is one of the most difficult tasks that can be imagined;
sustained self-clarification may only be an ideal which is never
reached. The encounter with others represents one of the important
mechanisms whereby we develop tools for meeting ourselves.

A group represents a small, manageable sample of the world,
and the group member's movement through that world is of prime
interest. His conduct within that world elicits responses and reactions toward him; eventually these add up to a set of expectations upon the part of others which govern a considerable part of
their behavior toward him. The individual's movement through the
group can be considered the *group career* and the reactions and
expectations the others have of him at any given time constitute his

group fate. Both group career and group fate are analogous to what occurs to the individual outside the group; because they are more manageable within the microcosm of the group the specifics of both career and fate are more easily examined. Because of this, it is important that each group member have as much freedom as possible to develop his career without prejudgment; under such a circumstance, knowledge about the individual which precedes the group experience is not necessarily an advantage and may hinder the clear development of a career based exclusively upon the individual's own idiosyncratic interaction rather than what has been imposed upon him. The relevance of the group career, in its own right, makes the here-and-now experience of the group extraordinarily valid data which, coupled with the immediacy of emotional involvement, creates a powerful learning experience. It is an important step toward meeting himself rather than a version of himself.

A group member brings to the small world of the group not merely a "phony" and "real" self, but a variety of selves, as suggested by the subself theory of Shapiro.[8] Basically any individual plays a large variety of roles within his world but generally permits only a narrow range of such roles to be exhibited in any setting.[9] The encounter group is an opportunity to explore the widest possible combination of roles in a particular place—it is especially when incongruous roles come together in the same person that problems are anticipated: the efficient executive and hurt child are seen as mutually exclusive. Having the freedom to permit both these to show within the same setting leaves the individual with a greater degree of spontaneity. Over time people come to have expectations of "the world"—an amorphous, unexaminable concept. One of the advantages of the small world of the group is that it becomes a reference group for particular roles so that expectations of consequences can be tested out against a specific reality rather than the vague and imaginary. The relationship between reference groups

[8] Shapiro, S. B. "A Theory of Ego Pathology and Ego Therapy," *Journal of Psychology, 53,* 1962, 81–90.
[9] This view of the group has been developed in considerably more detail in Stoller, F. H. "Video Tape Feedback in the Group Setting," *Journal of Nervous and Mental Disorders* (in press).

and the development of values, expectations, and goals has been explored by Turner.[10]

Very few, if any, ground rules are established for the group. It has been found that such rules are unnecessary and much of what is considered appropriate for the group can be modeled by the group leader—that is, demonstrated through his behavior. For the most part, groups are given an open, unstructured setting at the beginning, and out of the struggles which ensue the following group operations develop:

1. Accuracy of response—being "right" is downgraded over honesty and spontaneity. It is necessary to stress this early in the group experience, when people are beginning to know one another on the basis of fleeting and scattered data. It is likely, particularly at this phase, that the group will have an especially varied set of reactions to any given individual and group members are encouraged to contribute their unique reactions rather than wait until they know how the wind will blow. Consistency over time is considered no asset; the expectation is that people will change their reactions as they know one another more fully. Therefore, honesty, with all of the individuation that it implies, becomes highly valued.

2. Being reacted to rather than understood is a consistent group goal. Understanding implies explanation and speculation, operations which impede the encounter. Certainly the accumulation of historical data about group members as an aid to such understanding is strongly discouraged, just as elaborate defensive self-justifications tend to be dismissed as irrelevant. A distinction is made between the explanatory story and sharing, or permitting other group members to enter an experience that has retained its emotional potency for the group member.

3. Concentration is upon what is present within the group, the here-and-now rather than out-of-group data. This is a particularly difficult task to maintain and is, likely, an impossible ideal to reach completely. In actuality, it is likely to be the proportion that the group spends upon such material which is important and the

---

[10] Turner, R. H. "Role-taking, Role Standpoint, and Reference-Group Behavior." In B. J. Biddle and E. J. Thomas (Eds.), *Role Theory: Concepts and Research.* New York: Wiley, 1966.

emphasis may be a way of counteracting the overwhelming tendency of therapeutic groups to speculate over historical data, as Hill's[11] research has indicated. It is important that the here-and-now rule of the group be clarified since it does include the entire range of the emotional component which significantly resides in the individual at the time. What counts is not the content of what is being said but its effect upon others.[12] An account which attempts to shore up or clarify a stance produces a very different effect than an emotional sharing which helps bring others into contact with a new level of the individual. Encouraging a participant to move through an emotional residue such as grief or rage can help him to alter his functioning with others and to enlarge his contact with himself.

4. One of the most important group operations consists of giving feedback, the specification of the effects one group member has upon another. A key element in this is the immediacy of such information, as Benne, Bradford, and Lippitt have suggested.[13] Putting aside the benefits to the recipients of feedback for the moment, it places obligations and considerable opportunities for learning upon the sender. These can be categorized as follows: (a) the giver of feedback becomes more in touch with his own fleeting responses which, under ordinary social conventions, become discarded because they are rarely verbalized; (b) it is the obligation of the giver of feedback to specify, as clearly as he can, the basis of his reactions so that he must scan out his own inner state and perceptions more thoroughly than is generally the case; the consequences are that he sets into motion ways of encountering himself more fully; (c) through the range of observations (and lack of observation) the group member makes himself known to the rest

[11] Hill, W. F. *Hill Interaction Matrix.* Los Angeles: Youth Studies Center, University of Southern California, 1965.

[12] A parallel specification of the here-and-now containing within it residual emotions from the past can be found in Thomas, H. F. "An Existential Attitude in Working with Individuals and Groups." In J. F. T. Bugental (Ed.) *Challenges of Humanistic Psychology.* New York: McGraw-Hill, 1967.

[13] Benne, K. D., Bradford, L. P., and Lippitt, R. "The Laboratory Method." In L. P. Bradford, J. R. Gibb, and K. D. Benne (Eds.) *T-Group Theory and Laboratory Method.* New York: Wiley, 1964.

of the group in terms of how he perceives the world, his capacity for honesty or deviousness, and how he offers help; in short, the group learns about him through his behavior rather than through the version of himself he would like the group to buy.

5. It is in receiving feedback that countering can be seen in its clearest form. Ostensibly participants enter the group to learn about themselves so that, theoretically, receiving such information is in line with the goal. However, in practice, most people are searching for a counterblow at the time that the information is being presented to them; they cannot do this and consider it at the same time. To some degree the struggle with the group is essential in that it will tend to bring forth more data from others, whereas too ready an acceptance has the effect of getting the group off one's back. In receiving feedback, the following elements are important: (a) the feelings toward the sender of the feedback are of paramount importance and color, to a considerable degree, the nature of the counterblow so that exploration of relationships may be a prime consequence; (b) countering, or attempting to ward off the feedback, is important because it reveals, often in a sharply defined fashion, the inner dialogue that the recipient of the feedback tends to maintain with himself; (c) the appropriate self-searching attitude which might profitably accompany feedback by no means calls for ready acceptance but rather for considering, for "trying on" the feedback for its apparent relevance for the individual; when this attitude is manifest there is an actual physical strain which is apparent as the recipient searches himself and rejected feedback acts as a stimulus for other possibilities within rather than yielding the feeling of being taken off the hook.

6. Differential feedback from various group members occurs a good deal of the time. Within every group and for almost every participant there come times when a consensus is reached and he must face a powerful barrage from the entire group. This can become group pressure at its most persistent and forceful. Providing the group is not scapegoating at this point, no attempt is made to dissipate the pressure for two important reasons: (a) the group may be telling the individual something very important about him-

self in an extremely direct manner; (b) the pressures which impose upon all of us are made most explicit at this moment. Most people either succumb completely to pressure or unequivocally oppose it and it is only when they have had the opportunity to experience it clearly and see it through that they seem to have the option to deal with pressure in a more differentiated fashion—to pick and choose what they want to resist and what they want to accept; the free individual has the option to stand up against or go along with.

7. Finally the group must learn when words are superfluous, when contact and communication must be attempted on an entirely different level. Resorting to nonverbal techniques permits the group members to explore new ground, to risk what they ordinarily avoid. It also enables them to stop what they customarily do and allow other response patterns to emerge. Such techniques can easily become routinized for a group and, if used without sensitivity, promote sidestepping conflicts and difficulties rather than going through them. Nevertheless, the nonverbal approach can be an extremely important and potent dimension for the group to explore.

Listing the group operations in such neat fashion may make it appear that they develop within the group itself with such orderly regularity. The structure is imposed by the group leader and appears mainly in his conceptual framework. Within the actual arena itself there are ebb and flow, clash and deadlock, movement and frustration. Above all there is mutuality, the shifting back and forth between group members of the various group roles; the one who is attempting to help suddenly and unexpectedly becoming the recipient of help himself, the group member who has made a personal discovery turning around and aiding another member in developing his self-discovery. The major lines are always between the group members, with the group leader occupying a very special place.

Since the distance between what a practitioner says he does and what he actually does can be considerable, the group leader's conceptualizations of how he leads should be highly suspect. The importance of personal style is such that it probably accounts for more of what the leader actually does than volumes of lofty ideation. It is felt that the group leader should use himself, his own re-

actions, personality, and personal circumstances as readily as possible, as Shapiro has suggested.[14] In this manner the leader is a
group member, albeit one who has a special position. It is important to stress that personal style is extremely important; one
should manifest his own fashion of interacting rather than copy the
charismatic qualities of other leaders.[15]

While there is relatively little structure imposed upon the
group in terms of rules, techniques, or programs, the group leader
is not seen as a passive shepherd. Rather he leads by modeling;
instead of telling group members what to do or waiting until they
come to the appropriate operations by themselves, he illustrates
through his own behavior. Thus, if he would like group members
to react with honesty, he can show the way with his own honest
reactions; if he wishes group members to utilize feedback, he gives
feedback himself. The group leader helps set up an experience in
which a broad range of interpersonal events are likely to happen;
he does not make it happen but rather helps create the conditions
in which important things can take place.

Certainly an important function of the group leader is to
help group members utilize the group operations with the greatest
potential effectiveness. Another important function is the promotion
of risk-taking—entering areas which seem new and dangerous for
the participants. Risk-taking will most likely take place in an atmosphere of trust and the group leader has a specific role in promoting the sense of trust, not through his bedside manner but through
what he can show of himself under the appropriate circumstances.[16]
People develop expectations of one another depending upon what
they see, and the group leader is no exception. Unless he shows
himself, the expectations built around him will be based upon the

[14] Shapiro, S. B. "Myself as an Instrument." In J. F. T. Bugental
(Ed.) *Challenges of Humanistic Psychology*. New York: McGraw-Hill, 1967.
[15] A fictionalized version of group leader style can be found in Sohl,
J. *The Lemon Eaters*. New York: Dell, 1967, a novel describing a marathon
group experience.
[16] A broader discussion of the development of trust within the group
can be found in Gibb, J. R., and Gibb, L. M. "Emergence Therapy: The
TORI Process in an Emergent Group." In G. M. Gazda (Ed.) *Innovations
to Group Psychotherapy*. Springfield, Ill.: Thomas, 1968.

mythology of the leader or charismatic father figure—unrealistic and unduplicatable in the world outside the group. The group leader has the option of showing himself in how he deals with a personal crisis that arises within the group; his own honesty and strength in dealing with personal confrontation directed at him reveal a good deal of his capacity under stress. Given such knowledge, the group members have a better idea of what to anticipate from him should an acute crisis emerge within the group. Knowing what to expect from the leader, they can feel freer to take risks themselves. Above all, the leader must be honest with himself; otherwise, the group will sense a programmed self-presentation and will behave accordingly.

Utilizing oneself as an instrument precludes the mechanical use of technique. Anything that is programmed by the leader may move the group quickly but ultimately diminishes the growth potential of the situation. Programming implies preconceptions about what will be about to take place or slots within which people will be fitted which do not arise out of encounter and which are not able to be shared by all the group members. Utilizing co-leaders, while enriching the group experience, has a built-in danger; the leaders may consult with each other outside the group to solve, for their own satisfaction, situations which have arisen within the group or to resolve difficulties which have developed between them. When such outside solutions are brought into the group, members often have a sense of being "handled" and such maneuvers often backfire. Much preferred, despite its potential for arousing anxiety for all concerned, is consultation within the group and open resolution of conflict between leaders.

In one respect the group leader "manages" the flow of the group. With current microlab techniques, for example, it is relatively easy for a group to develop a cohesive feeling rather quickly: this is easily destroyed through harsh confrontation. Groups can peak too early or can bog down in frustration too deeply. It is the function of the group leader to help groups through this and the judicious use of techniques can be important. But ultimately, the group leader must design a *healthy* and *growth-inducing* way for himself to live and he must, both for his own sake and the sake of the people with whom he works, choose that which has the most thrust for himself. In doing so, he is also likely to have found the approach which is the most meaningful way for his own personal promotion of optimal group development.

A grand statement about the ultimate impact the encounter group could have upon the individual, the organization, and social style would be very tempting as a final flourish. It should be obvious at this point that this paper reflects a high order of enthusiasm for the basic encounter group. Yet to oversell it would be a disservice to an important experience with a powerful potential for transformation and growth. But the group is not life and life is not the group. There are built-in limitations to the process which emerge as people accommodate, become stylized in their group participation, and begin to use the experience as a way of warding off risk-taking. It is, in actuality, one of many important growth experiences through which an individual may go in his lifetime. The forms of the group are in a state of evolution, if not revolution, at the present time. The fact that methods proliferate should not be cause for despair; there will never be and should never be a *single* true road to the promotion of growth. What is needed is a richer array of opportunities for people to explore new dimensions in themselves and the world.

These phenomena exist over time rather than simultaneously and, therefore, are very difficult to illustrate without distortion or attenuation. However, it is important that we do ground these conceptions in actual events. The following fragment of a group experience encompasses a good deal of what has been discussed.[17]

Martin's participation throughout the marathon had been peripheral—he brought the group's attention to himself once or twice and made minimal comments to others. Saturday night he had left the group several hours early, exhausted (his investment in withholding) and with a bad stomach (dramatically linking the group career and group fate). When he was asked how he was on Sunday morning, he requested help in trying to make contact with himself. He felt that he eluded himself after a certain point. The

[17] This segment of a marathon group experience has been recorded on half-inch video tape. All names in this account are fictional.

group gave Martin feedback. It tended to be confused and diffuse (his real group fate); the most pertinent observation concerned his being exclusively "nice" and supportive. Martin agreed to everything that was said (a form of countering as evidenced by the lack of inner search and discomfort over taking in what was being said) and Martin's flow of words increased in proportion to his stalemate with himself and the group (illustrating an inner dialogue that was essentially avoidant—overtly he was seeking understanding rather than authentic reaction).

Frustration with Martin coupled with his acceptance of his homosexuality led the group leader to suggest that he be held down by several women (thus stopping the verbal flow, permitting something else to take place). Following this struggle Martin was clearly feeling strong emotions (showing the facility by which new responses can emerge when the customary is stopped). When he stated that they represented his struggle with his mother, Alice, who knew him outside the group, lashed out at his "dumping his problems on his mother" (it subsequently was evident that this feedback was revealing more of Alice). Martin started to back down when Mary asked if he really wanted to do that. Martin said, "No! It really was my mother!" (Alice was free enough to express her honest reactions rather than having to be "right"). He then began to cry. It was suggested that John, who had gone through an emotional crisis in the group, help Martin go through his (mutuality), and Martin was encouraged to talk to his mother in the form of a pillow (further exploration of action). When he began slowly, group members exhorted him to express himself more fully and, encouraged by them (a form of group pressure), Martin began to express powerful angry feelings, finally beating upon the pillow (suggesting what was available to him in the emotional here and now). Martin ended up weeping strongly on the floor following this angry outburst. This was then followed by Martin's going over to group members to physically embrace them in gratitude (the sharing was much more evident than the search for understanding).

When Martin reached Marilyn she refused to embrace him, stating that he had not really dealt with his mother, that she would still be able to get back at him and that she was only interested in a man (confrontative feedback). Others supported her and Martin began to manipulate the pillow, telling his "mother" to stay where he had placed her. As his insistence grew, Martin began to slam the pillow down and it burst open, spilling its stuffing all over the floor. Martin's delight was infectious as he rolled in the stuffing: "I did it! I did it!" The stuffing was over him, over the floor, and on everyone else. The group expressed pure delight. Martin returned to Marilyn for a genuine embrace and he continued around the group with profound emotional interchanges taking place (encountering). When he finally sat down, his face beamed (it was obvious that his internal dialogue could now be fuller, more honest, and more exhilarating than it was before). For Martin, the group had been both a backdrop, a dramatic confrontation, a powerful support and encouragement. He was now aware of aspects of himself of which he had only had the dimmest perception and had risked and gone through an emotional sphere that had largely been avoided. The incident helped other group members come in contact with aspects of themselves which they had only dimly recognized.

Within a forty-five-minute span this group shared, in addition to boredom and exasperation, exhilaration, despair, fear, risk, intimacy, contact, laughter and joy, pain and sorrow. Perhaps, ultimately, it was an experience in what could be.

VII

Poetic Dimensions of Encounter

Meyer M. Cahn

For a very long time, poets have given the world the very best feedback. Their poems have served as candid and descriptive statements incorporating feeling, cognition, and all that man can bring to his observation of other men and the world about him. And, of all verbal forms, poems are the most efficient. Their pithiness, and their maximum effect, out of a minimum of symbolic expression, would be approved in feedback circles anywhere. It is probably for this reason that some laboratories for human growth have set aside time for the reading of poetry. Somehow, the thoughtfulness and general tone of the poetic art fits the mood of commitment of the laboratory.

In a one-week lab, we set aside a half-hour one evening for a general session of poetry. It was held after dinner and before the evening group meetings. It was voluntary. It was at this meeting that I found myself reading two of my own poems, which had come out of the group activity of the previous twenty-four hours. These, in turn, led to some other activities and, I suspect, some future thinking on my part, on the matter of poetry in laboratories, feedback, myself as a poet and as a person, and other matters which can arise out of the dimensions of encounter.

I had not intended to write any poetry. What happened was that Stu Atkins and I agreed to ask our T-groups to cluster and observe each other for an hour or so. Except for this, we worked in our separate groups for most of the week. The group's observation exercise would offer the usual benefits of fresh feedback, comparative reflection, and an opportunity to try out new behavior. It would also offer an opportunity for us to see each other as trainers "in action" with our groups.

My group had been somewhat apprehensive about the proposal, and therefore discussed the joint session at length. His group was ready and accepted it immediately. They had been intensely at work on a problem of a young woman whose femininity was involved and, in fact, at stake.

When our groups met—his already seated in the inner circle—there was instant drama for all of us. Without any hestitant preliminaries, a dark-haired young lady named Beth explained that she had been reviewing the group's feedback since the afternoon session—"your horrendous feedback"—and going through some careful and rather painful introspection. The group listened in eager silence. I felt quickly involved. The feeling was thick and contagious. Her shaking voice, her commanding hold on our attention, and her words—"it struck me in my soul"—pointed out that her circumstance was far more compelling than the possible embarrassment of appearing in front of a new and strange group of people.

I was particularly interested in Stu's behavior, too. One of my strong motivations for joining our two groups was to see if I could catch some sense of his style. He was about three or four seats from her, his body in a strange tilt in her direction. When someone else spoke, he settled back slightly and turned toward the speaker. But soon again his body leaned forward and then swiftly he took an empty chair near Beth. In a moment, she was sobbing on his shoulder. It happened quickly and movingly. She sobbed deeply and unevenly; none of us knew when she would sob again, or if she might say something cheerful between the tears. People came up with Kleenex; Stu whispered to her as though none of us were present. He was with her all the way. It was a rather beautiful and intimate experience.

This event dominated the entire session—first, Stu holding her and really being with her through the tearful episode; then others commenting about this intimacy.

The next day I found myself writing a brief poem about it. As I say, I had not intended to. The poem dashed itself off quickly. When I finished, I realized that it provided another chance to see how I had experienced this event. At the time there was no title. The title arose later out of a discussion of the episode with Stu.

CELEBRATION

I saw you to the ready
A tight cat's jump from her
Her faltering voice, her words,
"It struck me in my soul."

And then you leaped to position
Your head upon her face, your cheek to hers
Your hand full holding neck, caressing
Soothing, together, oh together
Eyes closed, so together

Now she could sob, could well release
The child could be, the hurt pained out
The disjointed flow of life
Since held within, now out
With another. With you.

You deserve to be, whatever you are
A man, a friend, a paid servant
Who gives this way—
We all become; I mean become
Proud, safe, better
Even now, to think of it
Brings my own tears
But alone, they do not come.
They never do, not really
Unless there is a hand, a cheek
Another there to caress
Whose caressing says,
It is all right to be. It always is.
Especially now, it is.

When I showed it to Stu he read it carefully for some time. What he said was terribly complimentary, and I gladly accepted that. But there were other things that he did not say. He sat holding the paper, occasionally groping for words, and I felt that there was more going on within him than he managed to put into words. As we sat together, I realized the gulf that separates people, even those who have the best of intentions. Because he, too, is a writer, I could have accepted any kind of statement from him—the choice of word here, a clarification there. He did, in fact, suggest a deletion of one word. But the force of his attention was upon more personal matters, I believe. Perhaps he caught a new mirror of the event. Or something about himself. Or how he looked in the group. Or perhaps he was puzzling his relationship to me, and mine to him. We had met only four days earlier. Sharing the experience through a poem was a new experience for both of us.

I have written only a few poems in my life. All of them, incidentally, have been written during laboratories. I have taken note of this phenomenon in a previous paper.[1] This was the first

[1] Cahn, M. M. "Who Writes Doggerel? Or Poetry Even?" Paper presented at Human Relations Laboratory II, Bethel, Maine, June 28, 1968 (mimeo.).

time I had ever written about an encounter of this kind and certainly it was the first time that I had presented such an account to
the individual himself. The result enabled us to share a closeness to
each other and to the event. It also enabled me to have a referent
point when my own group asked some strong questions about my
behavior during the tearful event of the night before.

When our group reassembled in our motel room the evening
of the cluster, the behavior of one of Stu's group members was
challenged. She had been "inattentive." At a time like this, such
seeming disinterest made the observer "furious."

Then the attention was given to me. A rather large woman
turned toward me, caught my eye, and held my attention without
words. She smiled faintly, and then, shaking her head, she described
the anger she felt at me during the episode. And then with ac-
cusatory deliberation, "You had a smile—maybe it was a half-
smile, on your face. But boy, did that make me mad."

"Yeah," said another woman, coming up straight in her
chair. "I couldn't understand it."

There was a slight bustle of agreement and disagreement;
but the spotlight was unquestionably on me, now. A circle of eyes
passed my way and left no exit. I shook my head, my face even
now somewhat grinning. At the same time I could see that a few
worthies were ready to do battle for my side, too. "I guess I was
smiling," I said. "I even thought about it at the time."

When the embrace of Stu and Beth lingered, and because
we in the outer group were not allowed to participate, there was a
special opportunity to look around to the others, and there was
time, too, to consult myself and how I felt inside. I have not often
felt this way, but I knew that I felt good. It was a special moment,
this experience, with the off-balance of tears, the suspended feeling
of being caught in the impulses of the central actors. I knew this.
But I thrive on improvisation and, in this instance, there was something not only compelling about it, but there was a rhythm of
culmination, of ebbing out, that seemed to tell me that much had
gone on before that was ugly and difficult, and that the actors were
willing to put that behind them. There was a feeling of forgiveness,

and granting a new start and, for Beth, a hesitant but growing certainty that she would accept this new start. So during their embrace, during the aftermath of the tears, which was, after all, the longest part of the episode, there was a joyousness which I sensed and responded to.

But from the tone of our group discussion, the episode was a matter of grim business, at least to some members. Others accepted my expression. One of the more attractive women in the group, a young woman in her early thirties who had been fairly active from the first meeting, asked, "What kind of expression would have been appropriate?"

Perhaps I gave her too quick an answer. "I'll tell you, if you will give me the appropriate expression for an orgasm."

"I can't," she replied. "I never had one."

I thought about her answer, and wanted even to explore it, but this did not seem to be the time. On the following day, I did propose to the group that we might wish to talk about orgasm and how we viewed the whole idea of it, and what it might mean in general life terms. But we never got around to it. However, when I briefly bumped into the young woman informally, later that day, and the matter came up, she replied that her answer to the question was easily explained; "I have never been married." Rather than answering the question, this statement led to other questions. But these were private matters, and other things intervened.

That afternoon when Stu and I chatted, the poem offered me a chance to clarify that smile on my face during the episode. In our discussion, I realized that I have done a good deal of thinking about tears since spending that week in a group with Frederick Perls some five years ago. Never did I cry so much, or see so much therapeutic crying. It was the beginning of my interest in the relationship between withheld tears and aborted behavior. Beth's avalanche seemed like one of those basic events when tears of yesterday are finally spilled out, leaving room for new strength, and for a new view of contemporary reality. I said to Stu, "It was really a celebrative thing, a culmination. . . ."

"That's your title," he said. "Celebration."

Later that day, I placed the title above the poem. It seemed appropriate. Later, too, Beth came by and asked for a copy of it. She wanted Stu to read it to the group. She wanted a copy of it for herself, too. She seemed to value it.

In observing Stu during the joint group meeting, I realized that his was a style that incorporated much more "giving" in a personal and intimate manner than I have incorporated into my trainer role. Yet, I was very pleased with everything he did. The involvement, the "being there" to help the feeling become expressed, the good effect all this had on the group, and the satisfaction he himself received, all contributed to my unqualified approval of this trainer behavior, even if it was not in my own repertoire. Perhaps I wrote the poem because I wanted to recapture his behavior for myself so that I could understand it.

But when I returned to my own group, I was in no sense interested in emulating Stu. My style was different, I told myself. I was not interested in competing with him. Yet oddly enough, my second poem arose out of a situation not entirely unrelated to his behavior with Beth. Instead of Beth, it was about Mary. And instead of Stu, it was about me.

Mary was the one who had replied to my comment about orgasms, "I never had one." This in itself had been disconcerting, but tied in with other things, there was more to be concerned about. Not only was she unmarried, but here she was explaining to the group that she was about to resign herself to the fact that she never would be. Yet she wished marriage for herself. "I guess I'll be supporting myself for the rest of my life," she told the group.

Her admission of such defeat was inconceivable. She had been helpful to many members of the group, occasionally leaving her own position to sit near a beleaguered member, or to hold the hand of another. These gestures were done easily and with sincerity. But despite this, she could not now come to her own aid. She said that she just "wasn't worth bothering about," that she was "neutral," not good or bad, worthy or unworthy, just "neutral." She just did not feel it was worth our effort to support a good judgment of her.

Of all the people in the group, I felt that she displayed the best sense of the moment. She had the capacity to move her interests and feelings around the group. But there she was, demeaning herself, and now uncomfortable in the attention she was receiving, and certain that her poor judgment of herself was supportable. I felt that she was a good candidate for some "positive bombardment,"[2] and proposed this. She agreed to it, as did the group—which was eager to help her. So we set up an exercise where she stood in the center, and where two helpers and the entire group helped her to declare some of her virtues, strong points, good features, and good deeds. Though she was uncomfortable, I could see that she would go through with it.

I started it by reminding her that she had been the one to hold the hand of Jeanne during her hour-long trial with the group, the first person, by Jeanne's admission, to make this kind of contact with her in a very long time. She admitted to this. And then she sought to recall other virtues—but words did not come. So the group offered a few, but I doubt that she heard them. She looked straight ahead, her lips quivering. She tried to think of something. Someone said, "You're helpful." Then a pause. Her eyes were moist.

"You're attractive," I said.

Her quivering lips drew down painfully. Her eyes reddened. I could sense that something wanted to happen.

I arose and came to her. I put my arms around her, and she fell into them. Then I could feel her upheaval and her wet face against mine. Her chest moved upward several times, and now I could hear her crying. I held her close to me, my hand at the back of her neck. I pressed her head and closed my eyes. The tears did not matter.

There we were in full view of the group, but it did not seem to matter. For me, it seemed just right. I had not wanted to do this, yet when I saw her there, her body quivering, her search for release, I had the same need, too. So there we were together. And for some time.

[2] Otto, H. A., and Hansen, K. W. "The Multiple Strength Perception Method: A Four-year Evaluation," *Proceedings of the Utah Academy of Sciences, Arts, and Letters, 43,* 1966.

My mind was full of mixed flashes. At the same time that I meshed myself with Mary in this terribly inevitable circumstance, I was aware that my hand at the back of her neck was doubtless an imitation of what Stu had done the night before. Too, I thought of my adolescent peers whose influence on my behavior had always been strong, and how silly I must look to them now. But I was telling them privately to go to hell as I drew myself up to enjoy these new and mature prerogatives of mine.

Later, when the group talked about Mary and the matter of feeling one's sense of worth, I found that I had a stronger sense of indignation about all this than I had realized. My anger was leveled against those who provide harsh and unyielding judgments that become far too permanent and become translated into such actions as basic life disappointments (Mary and marriage) and fundamental notions such as who we think we are, even if the evidence is overwhelmingly to the contrary.

It helped me a little to say this in the group, but when some chit-chat dialogue threatened to replace the feeling of Mary's problem, I needed to keep hold of my feeling—my feeling for her, and my feeling of indignation. I decided then and there that I wanted to write a poem about this.

The poem, I knew, could offer an outlet. With the group going off into other directions, it seemed the only way that I could really handle what I felt. I privately debated leaving the group to do this immediately. When the subject changed, and my mood began to change with it, I decided to leave, casting my behavior into the category of risk behavior, something which is legitimate at almost any time, I told myself.

The poem came swiftly, perhaps in ten minutes. Then I returned to the group. But they did not hear it until that evening when we scheduled the voluntary general session devoted to poetry, attended by about 20 per cent of the delegates. At that meeting, we heard some Robert Frost poems on a record, and some of the delegates and staff read poetry related to the concerns of the week. I read "Celebration" and this one, along with a few others. Mary was not present.

MADONNA

Madonna, lovely one
From my eyes a warm vision
To have, and want, perhaps to love.
Outside, from where I sit
Yes, from here to love.

But inside, you recoil
From what I see, and others, too
You say there is no warmth
No thing to love. Just neutral.
This you say of yourself.
And even believe!

Who did this dastard thing
Who took this fair face,
This woman of grace and depth
Who made her feel this empty
And disregarded
Who did this thing had no right
In that day, even. But for other days?

For she goes on, belongs to all of us.
Not just those first
The ones who tore her away
Tore her in this way
Their robbing was too great
In time it did extend
So that they robbed not only her
But me.

How dare they take her from me
Me, they did not know
How dare they judge for me.
Her worth—but more,
How dare. How dare
They judge for her.

"Madonna" was well received. Perhaps too well received. Mary, who had not been present at the poetry session, had heard about it already, so that when the evening meeting of the T-group started a few moments later, she asked to hear the poem. Some of the other group members wanted to hear it and "Celebration," too.

I really did not want to read these poems in the group. I had already enjoyed sharing them with the people in the poetry session. It had been a moving experience for me to read them, to know that I was really being heard through them. Someone told me later that there was a real congruence between my voice and the sentiments of the poems. I knew this already because I felt it. But there is not always that congruence between what I say and how I say it. In this medium, I could readily achieve it. Perhaps this is where a good deal of "me" is.

I did not want to read the poems because I felt the group ought to work on its own stuff and not rely on the ready material of the trainer. Perhaps this is just second nature to me, now. Still, I did not want to avoid the experience, either, if they strongly wanted it. So I waited for them to ask again, and to indicate clearly that it was a group decision.

I went to my room for the poems. I saved Mary's poem for last. As far as the group was concerned, it was the one they most wanted to hear, mostly because of Mary, I suppose. When I read it, Mary was sitting to my left. As I read, she held her fingers tightly to her mouth; I could see that this was a very moving event for her. But she let me finish.

Then she came to me. I mean, she left her seat and kneeled down on the floor, and leaned against my knees. She was shaking her head as though to say no. She had difficulty saying what she wanted to say. Her tears and her shaking prevented the words. She seemed to be asking several things at once, and I was not sure whether I understood her or not. "Why did you do this?" she asked. "Why did you do this?" Did I tell the people in the poetry session about her? She needed to know how it was presented to the larger group.

The group tried to reply for me. We answered her and tried to let her know that her own identity had not been revealed. Still we wanted to be truthful about it. It had been introduced as coming out of "something that had happened in our group this morning."

Mary thought about this, and then her tears flowed stronger, her sobs deeper. She put her head on my lap and cried into it with a muffled sound. I put my arm around her head, then both hands, and I caressed her neck. I felt strange just sitting there. I knew, too, that my face did not show the same feeling that I had felt this morning when Mary and I were deeply embraced. My face was fully exposed to the group now. They were free to inspect it. But what they saw now was not a merging of our feelings, but two disparate concerns, separate, apart, and quite confused.

If I heard her right, she was telling me that I had no right to share this poem with any but her, that to do so was to violate her rights to privacy. I could sense that she could be right. But it was confusing because if she was right, then this power of saying things as you feel them, and saying them finally at this late time in my life, was again to be abrogated and frustrated. For I had waited until now, at this time, to be emancipated to the point where I could become filled with the feeling of an event, to where I could be free enough to say what I feel. And in my own way, this might not be final until I said it in an aesthetic form. For this is the way I have been ultimately expressive all my life: first as a composer, then as a short story writer, and now through brief poems. But it was wrong. Or at least it was not to be shared. Or was it?

It was quite confusing. But as I think of it, now, somewhat later, some matters are coming to light. For there is more to the issue than my right to create poetry. For one thing, I wish 1 had shared the poem privately with Mary before sharing it with anyone else. On a subsequent occasion, where a poem arose out of my encounter with a group member, I have asked for permission from that person before sharing it with others. But there are other matters, too. For all it is worth—assuming it is worthy as a poem—the poem is still a movement toward abstraction. It is addressed to everyone, and hence it is not directed to anyone, not really. Thus it cannot substitute for a direct statement, one made in confrontation, one person to another, their eyes meeting, their whole person at risk with the other.

The poem is on paper. It can be mulled over, crossed out, corrected, embellished—perfected. In fact, as I think of it, this poem was *not* a description of Mary, not exactly, not really. In making my statement, I was not primarily concerned with descriptive accuracy. I was concerned with effect. And so I thought of the word *Madonna* to insure the beauty of my subject, and followed it by the words *lovely one*. Did I feel that? Not quite. No, not quite. But I said it. I said it because when you write a poem you can do these things. You must. You dress the thing in order to make your case. Like mine and other people's, Mary's case is a fuzzy one. She is not the most beautiful woman in the world, nor is she quite as lovely as the poem would suggest. It just makes a better point to say that she is.

What I learned from Mary is that the poet is a phony—at least this poet. I learned, too, that you can not substitute a poem for feedback without running the risk of ruining the poem, or causing it at least to be ordinary and dull. To be authentic and on the mark, the poem may well have to make its point in lower key, and with greater subtlety than I would want to or be able to.

It was not fair for me to present Mary with so many compliments as though it were honest feedback. To make my case, I gave her a "fair face," "grace and depth," I said she was a "warm vision," a "lovely one," a "Madonna." In short, I was pouring it on. I trust she will forgive me. Almost all of these things are true, but in a different dimension. She is, as I say, as ordinary as the rest of us. And I was not in love with her. I was involved. Perhaps the truth is that the case I was making—this story of mistreatment —was really my own. Else why was I so moved to write about it— and so fervently?

There are several issues here. The first is my use of poetic expression as one more means of avoiding direct human confrontation. The poetic impulse comes to me at the very height of my involvement with people in circumstances which could be traced to my deepest concerns. By writing the poem, and by sharing the experience through the poetry, I have eluded the primary encounter of myself with the others.

On this point, I wonder if Stu's long and somewhat quizzical thought as he surveyed the poem "Celebration" was not in part due to his effort to find some separation between the reality I presented to him as a person interacting with him directly versus the reality I presented to him through the medium of my poetic expression. And I wonder the same thing about Mary, too.

A poem is a poem. It is not, at best, a direct statement from one human being to another. The two should not be confused. If one begets the other, they must still be looked at separately for what each of them is. It may be, too, that all of us are vulnerable to the fictionizing of our experience, that the poet in each of us fashions a pie-in-the-sky syndrome which gets confused with where we really are. The pie-in-the-sky comes out of a set of values which we can see with our own artist's eye, partly because we fashion it apart from the world of people. We fashion it with concepts, with records of other people's experience, with collections of our own past experience. We fashion it with abstractions which enable us to tell our story, much as the poet alters his world to tell his story. Behavioral scientists, who envision a special world of vastly improved interpersonal relations, organizational activity, and people whose lives are better because they know themselves more intimately, may also be confusing their poetic view with the view of the real world beyond them—the world each person has to live for himself —with or without the benefit of the poetic view.

The world is full of people who stretch their point in order to make it. Whether we call them liars, distorters, or poets, when we look more closely at their exaggerations, they turn out to have somewhat the same quality and goal—the quality of overstating the case in order to make the point. It is doubtless a ubiquitous human impulse that provides not only the great illusion of life which gives us such feelings as hope and joy, but also the basis for a later erosion because our reality was grounded on the vaporous myths of overstatement. And yet, where feeling is involved, who can be so precise? And who can present an accountant's ledger for his perceptions?

Our encounters, particularly those which are vivid and vital, will be rough hewn. We cannot tell each other perfect and moving poetry with rhythms, symbols, images, structures, and meanings flowing with inevitability and appropriate feeling. That means of expression is reserved for the poet who is separate and apart from the encounter of people with people. For the rest of us who are engaged with each other, our encounters will be imperfect verbal vehicles with their own rhythms, their own stops and starts. The words will be ordinary ones, the kind we use naturally—unedited. They will come without much pause, and certainly without much concern for aesthetic effect. They will at times have an unevenness, an overlapping, a fuzziness of meaning. At other times they will ring clear and will appear to have been designed by an artist.

It is tempting to try to ally the poem with the T-group, for both, as we have suggested, place high credence upon candor and both present a view of the world. Poems are about people and they are about the world. But they are art—apart from the maelstrom of life. The T-group is the maelstrom where people create the raw materials of the poem. It is people in their imperfection who are sometimes actually perfect—but only for so long. The poet can have a field day for himself taking note and deriving his aesthetic creations from that activity.

But he must remember—and I am saying this to myself, mainly—that his poem is not the real thing. People are. Eyes to eyes, breathing, touching, saying what they must say, responding, observing—all of these things in the rough exchange that brings us together trying to understand each other, with none of us excused from the process. None of us, including the poet.

After we contact one another, the poet's observation, as an observation, can make an interesting and rich addition. His is a vision—often beautiful, enticing, and terribly important. But it is only a vision. The rest is hard work, joy, and pain. To be sure, the poet's contribution adds more grist to the mill. But it is people—we people as people—who must grind the grist.

VIII

A Weekend of
Rational Encounter

Albert Ellis

My associates and I at the Institute for Advanced Study in Rational Psychotherapy in New York City have been experimenting for the past two years with various types of encounter groups in order to develop a procedure that would accomplish two main goals: first, to provide maximum encountering experiences for all the group members; and second, to include a good measure of cognitive and action-oriented group psychotherapy that is designed not only to help the participants feel better but also to get better. My chief co-worker, H. Jon Geis, and I have participated during this time in several dozen marathon and minithon groups and, in addition, we have conducted almost a thousand regular group therapy sessions. We have deliberately used a variety of techniques, ranging from the usual rational-emotive therapy procedures, which I have described in detail elsewhere,[1] to many of the highly experiential or expressive methods which are commonly employed in sensitivity training, basic encounter groups, and the marathon and group therapy procedures of George Bach, Frederick Perls, William Schutz, and Herbert Otto.[2]

We have finally devised and have successfully used a procedure which we call A Weekend of Rational Encounter. This procedure is more highly structured than the usual basic encounter and it is deliberately weighted more on the verbal than on the nonverbal side, although it does include significant aspects of nonverbal and action-oriented methods. It also gives a decidedly therapist-centered (as well as active participant) role to the group leader.

A typical weekend of rational encounter begins with the leader welcoming the participants, explaining to them that everything that goes on in the group will be strictly confidential and is to be subsequently discussed only with other group members, and that although the entire proceedings will be tape recorded, these recordings will be available for subsequent listening *only* by members of the group and for research purposes. He then asks each person to introduce himself and to answer the questions: "Why are you here? How do you feel at this moment about being here?" Each individual can be given a minimum and maximum of five minutes to present himself and forced to continue for this length of time (with prodding from the other group members); or he can be allowed to take as little time as he wants, and to run down before five minutes are up.

The group members are then asked by the leader the following one or two questions: (1) "What bothers you most right now,

[1] Ellis, A. *Reason and Emotion in Psychotherapy*. New York: Lyle Stuart, 1962.

[2] Bach, G. R. "The Marathon Group: Intensive Practice of Intimate Reaction," *Psychological Reports, 18,* 1966, 995–1002; Perls, F., Hefferline, R., and Goodman, P. *Gestalt Therapy*. New York: Julian Press, 1951; Schutz, W. *Joy*. New York: Grove Press, 1967; Otto, H. *Group Methods Designed to Actualize Human Potential: A Handbook*. Chicago: Achievement Motivation Systems, 1968.

either (a) in this group situation or (b) in your outside life?" (2) "What are you most ashamed of at present? Be as honest as you can be." While individuals are responding to these questions, other group members are permitted briefly to query them, to find out how they feel and what is going on inside them. But at this point the leader directively intervenes to stop any lengthy exchanges or detailed consideration of the problems that individuals bring up, since the purpose of the first part of the encounter process is to have all the individuals in the group open up about their feelings and attitudes and to give the other members some chance to know them before they cavalierly begin to respond to them or to try to help them with any of their problems.

If more opening-up procedures are needed, each group member can be asked: "What are the most important events in your life?" He or she can then be given from five to ten minutes to relate these events. Usually, however, it is found that this procedure is too prolonged and stuffy and that it brings out material that could better be elicited in another context. Often, moreover, this kind of historical material is irrelevant, leads away from the expression of current feelings, and gets the individual sidetracked into unimportant areas of his life.

The leader then says to the group: "*Look* for something right now which touches you emotionally (positively or negatively). Feel it. Report your feeling to the group." Several of the members may be called upon to express their feelings at this point; or all of them may be called. Calling on volunteers has the advantages of (a) bringing out unforced, genuine material; (b) saving time; and (c) smoking out, for possible later questioning and discussion, those inhibited members of the group who are afraid to feel or to express their feelings openly.

The group leader says: "Think of something risky you can do at this moment. Do it. Again, volunteers can be allowed to respond; or all group members can be forced to do something risky. If some remain silent, they can be asked: "Why didn't you think or do something risky after the other members did so?" (The group leader explains, at some point during the early stages of the weekend

or at this particular point, that members are allowed to do anything they like in the group as long as it is not physically harmful
to themselves or others. Breaking the furniture or jumping out of
the window, for example, is not allowed; taking off one's clothes or
calling someone names is permitted.)

The leader directs: "What member of this group would you
like to tell off? Why? Tell him or her off, right now." This procedure is normally done on a voluntary basis, since some people are
not hostile or do not as yet want to express any hostility. Silent
people can be asked why they did not feel like telling anyone off;
and very inhibited people can be forced, by the leader or other
group members, to tell off one or more of the others.

The leader says: "With what member of this group would
you like to have a love experience? Ask this person if he or she will
cooperate with you in having this kind of experience. If he or she
consents, engage in it as much as you can do, right now. If both
of you feel that you would like to have or to continue this love
experience outside the room, you may leave the group for a maximum of five minutes and have it in one of the other rooms of this
building. Be sure, however, to return after five minutes are up."
The leader then sees that (a) individuals having love experiences in
the room are asked about what they felt during the experience; (b)
individuals who do not choose to have love experiences with anyone
are asked why they did not choose to do so; (c) individuals who
choose to go out of the room for five minutes to have their love
experiences are asked, when they return to the room, to describe in
detail exactly what they did and what they felt while doing it. In
one way or another, all the members of the group are induced
either to have love experiences with at least one other member or to
report why they do not desire to have them.

This particular procedure is often found to be the most
moving and exciting one of the weekend encounter. It tends notably
to open up the participants to themselves and to others; it serves as
an entree into problem areas; it is usually risk-taking; and it tends
to make for experiential and therapeutic movement. If there is time,
it may be repeated later in the weekend (as may be any of the other

procedures which prove to be productive), with the proviso that the members choose a different person, this time, with whom to try to have a love experience.

The leader says: "Pick out someone in the group who you think might well be able to use some help with one of his basic problems. Sit in the center of the group with him and try to help him with these problems." All or most of the members are encouraged to work with at least one other member about his problems. Then the other members of the group, after watching and listening for a while, are encouraged to join in to help the individual whom the selector is trying to help. By the time this procedure is instituted, virtually all the members have had sufficient opportunity —usually over a period of seven or eight hours—to express themselves, to engage in some nonverbal (especially love) behavior, and to show what some of their problem areas are. They are therefore presumably ready for more detailed examination of their main problems; and this technique (a) encourages another group member to pick a problem which he thinks someone has, (b) intimately involves at least two members at a time in the problem-solving process, (c) gets many of the members, whether they like it or not, to go into more details about their thoughts, feelings, and behavior than they previously may have gone, and (d) actively gets around to the rational-emotive aspect of the weekend, with the therapist beginning to supervise the actual attempts of the members to help each other.

Up to this point, as noted above, the therapist keeps each participant's center-of-stage involvement fairly brief, to make sure that virtually everyone has a lot to feel and to express. Now he begins to allow from twenty minutes to an hour for each person to bring forth serious problems (or to have them elicited by others) and for him to work with an individual and with the group in a rational-emotive attempt to pinpoint and solve these problems. He often directly intervenes in order to teach the various members what the rational-emotive approach is: namely, that people are not disturbed as a result of the past events in their life at point A but by their own tendency to give certain irrational and disordered interpretations, values, and reactions to these events at point B. He particularly shows the individual presenting a problem, and the members of the group in general, how to distinguish and discriminate between their sane or appropriate reactions at B-1 (such as the beliefs that it is unfortunate and undesirable that various things have been or are now occurring at point A) and their irrational or inappropriate reactions at B-2 (such as the beliefs that it is horrible, awful, terrible, and catastrophic that these things have been or are now occurring at point A). He thereby indicates how they can retain their B-1 and minimize or eliminate their B-2 reactions, so that they significantly change their emotions and actions at point C. He also helps the members of the group to give activity homework assignments to individuals presenting problems—assignments which will help them effectively contradict their B-2 values and reactions, so that they get quite different emotional and behavioral results at point C.

For example, one of the women in a recent rational encounter group was shown, on several occasions, that she was only reacting as a therapist in the group, as she did in her own work with her patients, and that she was not revealing anything about her personal life because such revelations appeared to be too threatening to her. One of the males in the group chose her to work with and got in the center of the group with her in an attempt to show her how evasive she had been so far during the marathon. With some help from the rest of the group, he finally seemed to be reaching her, and she did admit that she had serious problems of her own but that she felt much more comfortable talking about other people's hangups than she did talking about her own. The group was highly elated, because this therapist member became quite upset, in the course of having her defenses assailed by the others, and began to cry and to admit that she really was, in spite of her seeming composure, a very lonely person, who mainly wanted to achieve a sustained love relationship with a man, and that she had miserably failed to do this as yet. They were all set to sympathize with her, to show her how therapeutic it was for her to admit her real problem, and to let her off the hook.

The leader insisted, however, that she right there and then look for the basic causes of her loneliness and her defensiveness. She said that she had been in psychoanalytic therapy for five years and that she knew these causes: namely, her rejection by her father, when she was a girl, and her insistence since that time that she find a man just like her father to love her and marry her. Her ex-husband and all her main lovers had been, on the contrary, weak men who were dependent on her, and who were not at all like her "strong" and rejecting father.

"Bullshit!" the leader interjected. "Even if these facts of your past life are true, they hardly explain why, first, you thought you absolutely needed your father's love originally, nor why, second, you are utterly convinced that you still need some 'strong' man's approval. What's the *philosophy* or *value system* that you in all probability had as a child, and are still holding on to, that *makes* you desperately in need of a rejecting man's love?"

This therapist could only come up with the idea that because her father had disapproved of her she now needed the acceptance of a man like him; but the leader insisted that this idea did not explain her original demand for her father's love. Finally, one of the group members said: "Don't you really mean that even when you were a child you strongly believed that if *any* significant figure in your life, such as your father, disapproved of some of your behavior that this meant that he thoroughly disapproved of *you;* and that the only way that you yourself could possibly accept your being, and think that you had a right to live and enjoy yourself, was if *all* the significant people in your life, including your father, indicated 'Yes, dear, we love you immensely, and we think that you are great!' "

"You're quite right," the troubled therapist replied, as she stopped her crying and began to listen to what the members of the group were telling her, "I couldn't even stand it, when I was young, if any of my girlfriends disliked me for any little thing I did. I thought I *had* to do it well, this thing, and *had* to be approved by them. And when I thought they disliked me, I hated myself."

"Yes," said another group member (who had thus far himself been defensive about bringing up his problems). "I know what you mean. I felt exactly the same way when I was a teen-ager. If one of my friends, or a parent or a relative, showed me that I was expressing myself badly or was acting impolitely, I either thought that they were accusing me terribly unjustly—or that they were right and I was an awful person! And I see, the way I am acting here today, that I still largely have this crazy view. Like you, I measure myself almost completely by the ratings that others make— or that I *think* they make—of me. I really think I'm a piece of shit if they don't think I'm the greatest thing that ever lived."

"I now see what you mean by my *philosophy*," said the troubled therapist. "I strongly believe that I cannot accept myself unless others first accept me—that I don't deserve to enjoy life unless they think I deserve to enjoy it."

"Right!" said the leader. "You have one of the main irrational ideas that create so much loneliness and self-deprecation in so many millions of humans: namely, that you don't merely *want* or *prefer* significant others to like your actions and prefer to be with you but that you absolutely, utterly *need* their acceptance in order to accept yourself. Now what can you do about minimizing this dire need and changing it back into a desire or preference?"

"Examine it, I guess. Ask myself *why* I cannot do what I want to do, or think I want to do, unless I have the approval of others."

"You're goddam right you can examine it!" said still another group member, who up to this time had been strenuously objecting to much of the rational-emotive analysis that had been occurring during the weekend and who had only wanted to go on having individual and group experiences. "And unless you do examine it and examine it, until you decide to give up this asinine philosophy, you'll continue to suffer from its results forever—as you have been doing right now, with us."

"Yes," said the leader. "Now let us see what kind of an activity assignment we can give you to help you combat your I-must-have-love-or-else-I-am-a-slob philosophy."

One of the group members suggested that this therapist, whenever she thereafter spoke up about others' problems in the marathon, also overtly and orally relate them to her own problems and to her own philosophies that lay behind her problems. She accepted this assignment, and carried it out for the rest of the weekend, and reported at the end that she was automatically beginning to see her philosophies much more clearly and to see how she could fight them and change them.

By the time the members of the group get around to discussing some of their serious problems in detail and to working with specific individuals and with the group as a whole in regard to these problems, the first day of the marathon—which usually lasts from about 10:00 A.M. on a Saturday until 2:00 A.M. Sunday—has expired. The group then leaves the premises and the members go home or to a nearby hotel to sleep, to talk, or to do anything they want to do. Although marathons were originally run on a twenty-four-hour or thirty-hour continuous basis, with members being forced to stay in the same room for that period of time and to sleep, if necessary, in the room itself, our experimentation at the Institute for Advanced Study in Rational Psychotherapy indicated that it is usually advisable to divide the marathon into two main parts, the first part consisting of about fourteen hours of continuous rational encounter therapy, then an interlude of about eight hours for sleep or relaxation, and then a resumption for another ten hours or so of therapy. This kind of procedure has also been found desirable by other marathon experimenters.[3]

When the group members return on Sunday, the leader usually starts off by saying: "We are now going to tell each other what each of us did last night and with whom we did it. How does each of us feel about what we did—or about what we wanted to do and didn't?" He may start off the round-robin himself, telling exactly what he did during the night and how he felt about doing it. He then sees that all the other group members, voluntarily or by direction, say something about their actions and feelings during the interim period. He can pursue this question by also asking all or some of the members: "What did you learn from your overnight experience?" "If the marathon weekend continued for another day and you had another night to spend before the third day, what would you now want to do during this night and with whom would you want to do it?"

Now that considerable time has passed and all or most of the

[3] Mintz, E. "Time-extended Marathon Groups," *Psychotherapy: Theory, Research, and Practice, 4,* 1967, 65–69.

group members have got to know each other reasonably well, two more round-robins are usually tried. First, the leader selects an individual to sit in the center of the room and all the other members who care to do so are encouraged to tell this individual what aspects of his behavior they definitely dislike and why they dislike it In turn, all the members of the group are forced to take this "hot seat" and to be told what their dislikeable behavior is. Second, the leader again selects an individual to sit in the center of the room and all the other members who care to do so are encouraged to tell this person what aspects of his behavior they definitely like and why they like it. In turn, again, all the members of the group are forced to take the center seat and to be told what their dislikeable behavior is. In each of these instances, each group member can be forced to comment on what he or she finds likeable and dislikeable about each of the other members. Since, however, this procedure is usually quite repetitious and time-consuming, when an individual is in the "hot seat" the leader can ask for only voluntary comments and repetitive statements about his dislikeable and likeable traits can be thus avoided.

In the closing hours of the rational encounter marathon, the group and the leader usually tend to smoke out anyone who has not as yet brought up any problem for detailed discussion. Such individuals are directly asked why they have not said too much about themselves previously and are induced to look for a major problem and to discuss it openly. In these closing hours, too, as mentioned above, some of the experience-provoking procedures previously employed can be deliberately used again. The leader can institute these procedures himself or may consult with the group about repeating them. One of the main purposes of trying them again is to see how much growth and development has taken place in the group members, especially some of the more inhibited ones, as far as certain expressions and actions are concerned.

In the closing hours of the marathon, there can be round-robins on these questions: (a) "What are a few of the most important experiences you have had during the marathon and the most important things you have learned about yourself?" (b) "In thinking about your marathon experience, what are some of the things that you did not say to the group or to individuals in the group when you had the chance to do so previously? Say these things now."

For the final half-hour or so of the marathon, the leader selects one member of the group at a time, has him sit in the center of the room, and says to the rest of the group: "Anyone who can think of a suitable homework assignment to give *x* that might help him to solve some of the problems raised here or to live more happily and creatively in the future, suggest this kind of an assignment right now. Let *x*, if necessary, take notes about these assignments, so that he will not forget them."

After the marathon weekend of rational encounter has ended, a date is set for from six to ten weeks ahead, at which time the group members are invited to return to the orginal setting for about four hours, to discuss what they think they got from the original marathon, what changes may have been effected in their lives as a result of it, how they carried out (or failed to carry out) the homework assignments that were given them, how they feel about participating in future marathons, and other questions of this sort.

This, then, is the basic procedure of a weekend of rational encounter. As can fairly easily be seen, it differs from most other kinds of basic encounter marathons in that (a) it is more directive; (b) it tries to encourage the group members' experiencing as much meaningful involvement with each other as they can possibly experience in a necessarily limited period of time; (c) it begins, largely, with expressive-emotive-experiential procedures but winds up, as a result of conscious planning, with concerted problem solving; (d) it is designed to be specifically therapeutic and not merely pleasure-inducing or experience-producing; (e) it includes a great deal of rational-cognitive and behavior-action methods, especially in the last half or two-thirds of the marathon; (f) it is run by a group leader who is a trained psychotherapist and who is therefore capable of helping, and preventing harm coming to, reasonably disturbed participants; and (g) it makes no pretense of including only "normal" individuals who desire more growth and development in their lives but also includes distinctly disturbed individuals who specifically come to be helped with their problems.

A weekend of rational encounter is specifically designed to answer most of the realistic objections that have been often raised against sensitivity training and basic encounter methods of organizing and running marathons in what has been called the human potential movement.[4] Let me now list some of the main objections to see how they are answered by the rational encounter methods:

The movement may be psychologically irresponsible, because it helps break down the defenses of some disturbed individuals, opens them up without closing them, and may lead to more harm than good. Rational encounter helps the individual to become less defensive by getting him to see, attack, and surrender his basic self-defeating philosophies or values which cause him to become defensive. It opens up and then makes a distinct effort to close and change marathon participants, so that they can usually lead more effective future lives—or receive further rational-emotive therapy which will help them do this.

The basic encounter group is anti-intellectual. Not the rational encounter group. Rational, cognitive, and intellectual processes are strongly encouraged; and, as in regular individual and group rational-emotive therapy, participants are taught how to question and challenge their own assumptions and how to use the scientific method in their everyday life.

The movement can breed narcissism. Narcissism or childish grandiosity stems from the irrational idea that only the individual is important and that the world should basically revolve around him. In rational group encounter the participants learn that this is a silly idea, that the individual normally has to live in some kind of social group, that he can become quite individualistic (that is, self-interested) and also live comfortably in his social milieu, and that his being considerate of and loving others is usually in his own interest and is not incompatible with his being himself. He is shown that the

[4] Howard, J. "Inhibitions Thrown to the Gentle Winds," *Life*, July 12, 1968, 48–65.

basic rule of morality is "Be true to yourself and mainly look out
for your own interests," but that its close corollary, for anyone living
in a society, is "Therefore do not needlessly harm other human
beings, and try to get their acceptance and cooperation, so that you
can live in the kind of atmosphere which is most beneficial for you
and your loved ones."

*The feelings induced in encounter groups frequently do not
last and cannot be transplanted in the soil of real life.* Rational
encounter does not merely induce feelings for their own sake—
though that is pleasurable and lovely and there is nothing wrong
with it. Instead, it follows up feeling with cognitive understanding
and restructuring and with behavioral activity. Consequently, its
results do tend to last. It does not, moreover, encourage expression
of overt hostility for its own sake—which may lead to inappropriate
subsequent expressions of hatred in real life. Instead, it induces the
admission of hostile feelings—and then clearly shows the group
member what irrational ideas he is telling himself, at point B-2, to
make himself foolishly hostile, at point C. It also shows him how
he can change his hostility-creating philosophy, so that in real life
he will tend to be considerably less hostile to his mate, his employer,
his children, and other close associates.

The movement breeds a kind of "emotional elitism."
Whereas many encounter groups deify feeling over thinking (which
they wrongly refer to as "intellectualizing" or "rationalizing"), the
rational encounter process strives for a reasonably equal balance
between emotion and cognition, and it demonstrates that some
emotional states are highly inappropriate and self-defeating, and
would better be changed by modifying the ideas and values that
lie behind them. At the end of a rational encounter marathon, the
participant tends to become more emotionally released and more
productively thoughtful about himself and the world.

Encounter groups can be used for brainwashing. In rational encounter therapy, the individual learns (as he does in rational-emotive therapy in general) to check and challenge his own
assumptions, to think more independently and clearly, and to use
the scientific method of taking his premises as hypotheses—rather
than as facts—and insisting, before he retains them, that empirical

evidence be shown to support them. He thereby becomes less con-
ditionable, less amenable to group persuasion, less direly in need
of approval and success. His original parental and societal brainwashing—to the effect that he has to keep proving himself to others
and that he is no damned good unless he is inordinately achieving—
is "brainwashed" by the group therapy process; and he becomes
less amenable to future brainwashing by any individual or group.

The human potential movement is too gimmicky. Certainly,
rational encounter is not. The leader's instructions to the group—
as can be seen from the material presented above—are exceptionally
simple, direct, undramatic, and brief. The "gimmicky" techniques
of physical exercises, sensory awareness, dancing, swimming, music,
strobe lights, group hand-holding, finger wrestling, and various
other "artificial" methods that are commonly employed today in
encounter groups are rarely employed (though there is no reason
why, if time is available, they cannot be supplementarily used).
Practically all the things that are done are the same kind of things
that would be enacted in everyday life—although they might not
ordinarily be practiced openly, in the midst of a group process.

The encounter group is too hedonistic. In rational encounter, the participants normally tend to enjoy themselves and to
be very much involved in what they are doing. Primarily, however,
pleasure of the moment is not allowed to interfere seriously with
business. The main purpose of the marathon is to help individuals
understand themselves and to be more able to effect significant
personality changes in themselves. Although pleasure, and physical
satisfaction in particular, are viewed as being good, it is not assumed
that merely having such pleasure is remarkably therapeutic. It is
assumed, rather, that human beings usually have to work hard and
consistenly at comprehending and modifying their irrational philosophies of life and that they had better be to some extent shown
how to do this kind of work during the marathon process and encouraged to keep doing it subsequently in their actual lives.

*The basic encounter or sensitivity training process is too
diffuse and inefficient.* It often, in my opinion, is. Letting disturbed, or even relatively "normal," group members largely mull
around in their own juices, and nondirectively explore each other's

feelings and thoughts while trying to get out their own inner emotions may often, in the long run, lead to some excellent results. But
it is so wastefully time-consuming in many instances! And it frequently results in a twenty-four- or thirty-hour marathon (not to
mention an entire week or two of continuous sensitivity training
sessions) where (a) some group members say practically nothing,
(b) few serious problems are intensively explored, and (c) much
time is spent in unimportant and irrelevant chit-chat. Rational encounter marathons are particularly designed to eliminate this kind
of inefficiency, to utilize almost every minute of the available time
effectively, and to draw in, both experientially and in terms of
important problem solving, virtually every member of the group.

*In the long run, the human potential movement is anti-
therapeutic.* This may well be true for certain aspects of the movement, just as it may be true for certain aspects of the taking of LSD
and other drugs. For human beings seem to become happier, more
creative, more self-directed, less anxious, and less hostile when they
change some of their basic irrational and childish assumptions:
especially the assumptions (a) that it is a dire necessity for them
to be loved or approved by virtually every significant other person
they encounter; (b) that they should be thoroughly competent,
adequate, and achieving in all possible respects if they are to consider themselves worthwhile; (c) that people as a whole, including
themselves, are bad, wicked, or villainous when they behave un-
ethically and that they should be severely blamed and punished for
their villainy; and (d) that it is awful and catastrophic when things
are not the way they would like them to be and when their desires
are not immediately gratified. These unrealistic and silly philosophies
or value systems are not only uncontradicted by many encounter
groups, particularly those of the conventional sensitivity training
type, but are actually sustained and enhanced by these groups.
Certain Esalen-type and Synanon-oriented marathon groups, for
example, wittingly or unwittingly teach their participants that they
are worthwhile people if other members of the group will give them
a bear hug or that they should enrage themselves at other marathon
participants who act impolitely or negatively. The rational encounter weekend, however, is specifically designed to show group

members what their fundamental self-defeating philosophies are and to indicate how they can work at changing these philosophies, in the here and now and thereafter. It is consequently a therapeutic experience that is oriented toward experiencing and behavior modification, toward self-expression and the specific teaching of new personality skills.

Is the rational encounter weekend the last word in marathon group therapy? Most probably not. We are still experimenting at the Institute for Advanced Study in Rational Psychotherapy with improved marathon procedures, and will doubtless come up with something a little different from what we now have. But we already have some evidence that the procedures we are using are far more efficient, in terms of concentrated experiencing of oneself and one's fellow group members, and in terms of acquiring saner and more creative ways of living in the world, than any of the other basic encounter methods that we have yet employed. Our last marathon at the Institute, consisting of sixty participants divided into four groups, produced both temporary and permanent results which were distinctly superior to those produced by any of our previous marathon procedures. We hope that, with continued experimentation, our future rational encounter weekends will even be better.

IX

Encountering and Groups

Thomas P. Malone

Psychotherapy is an intimate relationship between two or more persons encountering one another in ways new to each so that selves grow. When the experience of self expands naturally, which means interpersonally as contrasted with chemically or toxically, the self develops an associated increase in capacity for involuntary engaging, encountering, and intimacy. What follows describes only the general qualities of encountering as I have experienced it, as well as some beginning effort to describe the general conditions of its occurrence, particularly as these are found in group psychotherapy.

To begin, I will share the subjective dimensions of encountering. You may recognize them; they may be unique to me.

The best days I have as a psychotherapist are the days when I wake in the morning with a real feeling of aliveness and awareness. My deepest awareness at these moments is of myself, but the environment, the sun, the moisture on the ground, my breakfast, my children, my wife, the color of my car, all seem to be in sharper focus. There is no sense of having to see, of having to seek out my environment. On these days, my patients have this same quality of vividness. The humanness of the patient comes to me vividly. There is no sense of straining to see, or hear, or understand, or give, or reassure, or admonish. Paradoxically, it is most as if I am not paying attention to them, but am with myself. The paradox, of course, is that in these moments I hear, see, and feel them most clearly. There is no feeling of having to hear, or having to take care of, or having to understand. The patient seems more articulate and sensitive.

I am not describing simply a good, warm, affectionate loving feeling. Some of the feelings may, indeed, be negative. The chastisement, embarrassment, shyness, criticism, or even anger, however, feels definitive and lucid. The flow between is open and versatile, emergent and phasic. Time flies or stands still; it does not plod along. There is enjoyment. We learn together. I have rarely kept this feeling for an entire day, and only seldom have I kept it for a morning or afternoon. The tyranny of response intrudes, and the intrusion is insidious. I first feel an almost imperceptible slowing down of the flow and a slight blunting of the emotional clarity. I find myself beginning to pay attention to the patient. Almost immediately he becomes less vivid perceptually. Emotional noise distorts the clear tone. I sense a straining in both of us, accompanied by a sense of expectancy, which is not particularly enjoyable. The experience of mutual enjoyment recedes slightly. About this time, I begin feeling that the patient is now expecting, not yet demanding, a response from me. Not usually a particular response, but some response. Since I had been responding freely and involuntarily, the expectation of a response is felt as an intrusion. I feel a little irritated. This irritation is rapidly replaced by the assumption of a cultural posture in me, suggesting that he both deserves and needs a response. My business, then, is to ascertain specifically what response it is he is expecting. By this time, most of my involuntary responding has disappeared. I am confronted with someone in need, to whom I can only respond voluntarily. I usually do. The patient appears dubiously satisfied. I am clearly aware, however, that we have both accepted fairly standard cultural positions with each other, and that we now have no personal encounter. What we had had was the beginnings of the one-to-one encounter.

Encounter literally means to be *in against*. To be in against superficially has a conflictful implication. More deeply, however, it is a very warm image. In this latter sense, it is physical, deeply personal, tactile, meeting, not nice nor careful, exploratory, sensual, but not necessarily sexual. The word *snuggly* occurs to me. It most clearly is *not* culturally programmed. When one is in against someone, one does not spend too much time concerned with social or cultural postures. The being with is apt to be quite personal. The personal, sensual, nonprogrammed quality designates the essence of the encountering experience.

Encounters are passionate experiences. Behavior, whether words or activity, may be confronting, communicating, responding, or initiating. The experience becomes encountering only when it is passionate. Sharing feelings with another is not necessarily encountering. A broad spectrum of our feeling experiences is subject to detailed cultural programming. Furthermore, the passionate experience is not synonymous with depth or intensity of feeling. A culturally programmed feeling can be quite intense—for example, homicidal feelings, or a massive depression. It is the quality of the feeling that makes it passionate. The passionate feeling has minimal cultural and maximal personal programming. I realize, of course, that these are inseparable, but in experience the quantum of each varies. In the passionate experience, there is a high personal thrust. For example, feeling afraid when physically threatened would have a high personal thrust, in contrast to feeling embarrassed at your failure to remember an acquaintance's name, which would have high cultural thrust. The passionate feeling appears as pure, in the specific sense that it is feeling with minimal meta-feeling accompanying it. By meta-feeling, of course, I mean a feeling about a feeling. For example, you may be sexually excited, which is a dominantly personal feeling; if you feel vaguely ashamed of that, this is a meta-feeling. To complete the cycle, if you are ashamed, and do not even feel sexually excited, that is a neurotic feeling. The passionate feeling is apt to be unencumbered by such feelings as guilt, shame, embarrassment, condescension, or any one of the hundreds of others of what William McDougall called the *sentimental feelings,* that is, feelings which are either moral or immoral, in contrast to the passionate feeling, which is basically amoral.

The passionate feeling, because it has minimal cultural programming, subjectively does not require response. When I experience a passionate feeling, I am not aware of any need for the encountered person to respond, nor to create in the other person any compulsive sense that he has to respond. In this sense, it embodies remarkable emotional freedom. Although the passionate feeling encounter does not compulsively demand response from the other, passion almost always elicits response. This is its beauty. Passion elicits passion not because of its compulsive message, but because passionate feeling is generally contagious. The contagion does not create necessarily the same passionate feeling, but elicits feelings of a passionate nature, whether they are the same feeling or not. In addition to its purity, its lack of compulsivity, and its contagiousness, the passionate feeling lends itself to phasic experience. Since the cultural programming is minimal, the phasing of the person in and out of feelings on the passionate level is facilitated. The angered loves more easily without the usual awkwardness of the ambivalent person.

I have described encountering as a passionate experience. In contrast, neurotic feeling, in my experience, almost always includes meta-feelings, almost always compulsively demands response, is seldom contagious, and tends to perpetuate itself and precludes the phasic quality. These are clearly antithetical. The passionate experience can then be described as a feeling encounter with minimal neurotic intrusions. However rare, the passionate experience appears to be more nearly the natural experience, in contrast to the statistically more common but less natural neurotic experience.

I have described the encountering experience as essentially passionate, phasic and flowing, gratifying and enjoyable, essentially involuntary, novel, neither highly culturally programmed nor anticultural, but essentially personal, and more natural than neurotic. Since I consider growth natural, and deadlocked growth as neurosis and therefore unnatural, it follows that human experience that is natural facilitates growth. In this sense, the encountering experience looms as critical in psychotherapy.

Although most of my professional work is done in the one-to-one psychotherapeutic relationship, the group experience clearly better enhances the probability of the encountering experience occurring. The traditional one-to-one relationship has characteristics, both inherent and accidental, that is to say historical, which make the encountering experience very difficult, and even unlikely. The one-to-one relationship is very specifically defined in our culture. This cultural definition of the relationship between therapist and patient constitutes a serious obstacle to the encounter. The culturally defined relationship of patient and therapist has as its historical and current model that of the doctor-patient or priest-patient. Such a highly programmed relationship is not only obstructionistic, but antithetical to a process of psychotherapy, which is considered an emergent sequence of encountering experiences between, or among humans. Bluntly, the medical model emphasizes pathology in contrast to the encountering which emphasizes health and growth. The medical model emphasizes knowledge, particularly of the diseased other, in contrast to the encountering model which emphasizes feeling and awareness of healthy self. The medical model emphasizes technique; encountering emphasizes spontaneity and natural response. The medical model emphasizes, as it should, responsibility for other in the relationship, in contrast to the encountering model, which values responsibility for self in the relationship. The one-to-one relationship of therapist and patient almost inescapably takes on the characteristics of the medical model within the mind and feelings of both participants. The ensuing concern with pathology, emphasis on knowledge of disease, and preoccupation with technique makes the encounter in such a relationship unlikely. The fact that the responsibility for what occurs in the relationship resides in the doctor-priest person makes the encounter in such a relationship more of a miracle than a probability.

The significance of the encounter in psychotherapy increases

as psychopathology is seen not as a personal disease, but as an interpersonal event which, when actualized, is actualized between or
among people just as it originated not in but among people. To be
maintained, it has to be continually reinforced. Without interpersonal repetitive reinforcement, it would extinguish. In this sense,
the admonition of classical analysis not to get involved with the
patient's sickness was an effort to minimize this reinforcing interpersonal process. It has been unfortunate that it also limited the
therapist's freedom to be with the patient as a human being. That
is to say, it limited encountering, and thus healing. The sense
of enjoyment, excitement, aliveness, and the personal gratification
which accompanies encountering were designated as unprofessional.
This attitude removed from the therapist a very important option.
Encountering depends on the therapist's having the option to have
no response, as well as the option to respond passionately. Blind
attention to technique or professionalism, compulsive attention to
pathology, and programmed responding out of a sense of responsibility for the patient minimize encountering.

I have been describing the general qualities of encountering
as I have experienced it, some general conditions of its occurrence,
and a rationale of its significance in therapy.

I have said that in the one-to-one relationship, an encounter
is a miracle. In the group it is quite probable even with the same
therapist. Why? A singular advantage of the group which, in many
ways, was historically fortuitous, is that it automatically makes the
medical model of the therapeutic interaction somewhat inappropriate. The terrible disadvantages of such a model are partially modi-
fied. I know that some therapists are so engrammed with the model
that they can succeed in transposing a group into a set of one-to-one
medically modelled parallel relationships with the therapist radially
relating technically to a group of diseased patients who are a group
only in the sense of their being present at the same time in the same
place, related only to God or the therapist depending on their
theological tastes. But that is not group psychotherapy. As group
members interact with each other and with the gestalt of the group,
the therapist who is medically and culturally programmed gets confused, morally disoriented, and anxiously inappropriate. Things

begin to happen that were never described by William Osler or anticipated by the Hippocratic oath. These happenings are the rumbles of encounters. And strange to relate, these happenings have a way of developing their own emergent thrust in groups so that even the therapist who considers personal encountering somewhat sinful finds his disease-oriented philosophy, technical security, and compulsive sense of responsibility either disregarded or ignored. Usually he retreats to an inane defensiveness and ultimately discards groups as a therapeutic experience, or more happily says what the hell and begins enjoying his work as a therapist, much to the patients' delight and benefit. Parenthetically, he then usually has a year or three of overboarding with the joys of relating until he centers back in with more respect for ego function. But groups do naturally breed encountering. The group experience is more passionate, and certainly less hysterical than the one-to-one dyad.

In addition to not fitting the medical model, groups also diffuse that lethal sense of responsibility for others, which is so detrimental to encountering. The tyranny of response is challenged. The therapist has the option of not responding. His capacity for involuntary encountering correspondingly increases. The therapist's lessened sense of responsibility in the group has another consequence. Buddha is reported to have said in answer to a man who was raging angrily at him, "I don't know why you are so angry with me—I have not been taking care of you." The not-taking-care of feeling in groups leaves me markedly less angry. And therefore, less defended and open to personal dialogue or encounter. This relative absence of anger in groups in both myself and the patients, which I attribute to the group rather than any one individual in it becoming the caretaker, makes room for encountering. The aggressive experience is purer without the compulsive attacking negative exchanges which are so characteristic of the group gone sour, usually because one patient in the group has succeeded in making the rest of the group feel responsible for his pain and failure. Fortunately, group dynamics make such impasses difficult, in contrast to the ease with which they develop in the one-to-one, even though there the hostility is usually expressed more genteelly or professionally.

I have described the encountering experience as passionate

and the passionate experience as phasic. The phasic quality is a quality of natural feeling experience. It reflects the ease of movement within the feeling experience arising out of the absence of cultural programming or compulsivity. It makes role playing of feeling difficult, and the neurotic perpetuation of transferred feeling unlikely because of the lack of any sustained counterneurotic response. It is as if sheer numbers interfere with neurotic interactions taking shape. Someone seems to be always upsetting the applecart with a beautifully inappropriate natural nonneurotic feeling response. The phasic quality invites encountering. It enhances the individual's capacity to move from the excitement coming out of self to the quieter close intimacy with another. The capacity to phase from the involvement with self to the loss of self in the feeling of another describes encountering.

Oddly, groups are less culturally bound than the one-to-one relationship. The privacy of the one-to-one seems to invoke cultural taboos more strongly. The privacy becomes hesitant and stilted and leads to progressive spasms of cultural postures. The final tableau is of two persons playing roles stiffly, suffocating the encounter. Since the encounter and the cultural posture are antithetical, the relative freedom of the group from tight cultural programming creates readiness for encounters in the group. This is particularly true of the erotic encounter. In the one-to-one relationship, the erotic relationship is almost impossible, except hysterically. Even if it begins as a natural sharing, the meta-feelings, the transference thrust, and the cultural intrusion gradually reshape it hysterically. The simple capacity to touch in the presence of others allows the natural sharing to move to encounter without any hysterical detours.

Perhaps because of greater freedom from cultural intrusion in the group, interaction among its people is usually more physical, tactile, active, "do-oriented." Instead of verbalizing anger, the patient is apt to bang on the table; instead of simply feeling tenderness, the patient is apt to touch the loved one. I recently redecorated one of our group meeting rooms. The patients brought decorative objects enthusiastically. They were almost irrespressible in their desire to construct a large coffee table which I was having difficulty locating commercially. I would have accepted it, but they wanted to build a form, and pour the colored concrete in the room itself. They were alive, enthusiastic, and action-headed. I initially described encountering as the physical imagery of being in against— and this physicalness as a surrounding quality accompanies all encountering, even though most encounters do not involve overt activity. Even to the unspeaking, unbehaving encountering person, however, the experience feels physicalistic. The physicalness and activity I am describing differ radically from the acting-out set, which feels driven and automated. Again the enjoyment distinguishes it—a uniquely quiet enjoyment.

The readiness of people in groups to do provides them with a thrust to reality. The unique physicalness of the encounter provides the same thrust to reality. This designates one of its qualities, which creates a platform for self-growth and distinguishes the encounter from the symbiotic emotional experience so frequently confused with it. Emotional symbiosis is sentimental, not passionate. A common example is a therapist sympathetically reassuring a depressed patient.

Because of the thrust to reality, encounters facilitate ending. In the encounter, there is an experience of another human without a sense of dependence. It is a peer relationship in humanness. Again we find the same reinforcement between the group experience and encountering. The group characteristically facilitates ending and lessens dependence, as does the encounter.

I finally would like to suggest that one cannot encounter sickness, nor can you encounter with sickness. The encounter, by definition, is a healthy experience, perhaps a health-giving experience. This is true even if the person relating out of his health has considerable sickness in his person. The concept of encounter thus implies a basic assumption in psychotherapy—that of growth. Growth as change means the isolation and enhancement of the residual health in a patient, disregarding the sickness relatingly, although cognitively we may be constantly aware of it as interfering, impassing, and subjectively as non-health. Although I would have few agreeing, I would go so far as to say that psychological sickness per se is unalterable, except as it is overwhelmed by the growth of the health of a patient. Again it is my experience that in groups, people have less interest in sickness and more response to health.

Clearly I consider group experience the most fertile field for the therapeutic encounter. Simply bringing a group of patients together does not mean encounters will occur. The crucial variable remains the person of the therapist. Some therapists engender encounters in one-to-one relationships readily and frequently. Some therapists prohibit encountering even in active groups. The most suggestive observation is that therapists who do encounter and accept its significance in psychotherapy tend toward group involvement. Those who do not, but appear technically oriented, shy away from group experience. Personally, I renew my capacity for encountering when I am in group. This carries over to my one-to-one relationships, where encounters are admittedly more difficult. And I hope these generalize to my life where encounters are even more difficult.

X

Encounter in Community

Erving Polster

A short time ago a friend's son had just finished his work for his bachelor's degree. He is a social and political activist who had once been interested in psychotherapy. I asked my friend whether her son was going to become a psychotherapist and she said no, he thinks psychotherapy is irrelevant.

The ambiguity of this indictment opened my speculations about what he could have meant. I thought he might, as an activist, just have a point. The speculation I liked best is that the boy is a utopian thinker and he does not sense this kind of thinking among psychotherapists. To be sure, there are some writers close to psychotherapy who have been trying to put Utopia back on the map;

but they are few. The ones who first come to my mind are B. F. Skinner, Paul Goodman, and Martin Buber. Although none of them characterize themselves as psychotherapists (though Paul Goodman spent many fruitful years as one), their work has been central to current psychotherapeutic thought.

Skinner's *Walden II,* which fantasies the ideal community, is based upon his principles of learning.[1] In it the hero takes seriously the proposition that what we learn in the laboratory or with individuals can be applied to the cause of living a good life in an actual community. While you or I might differ with certain premises, Skinner's hero at least puts himself to the test of creating the utopian community, thereby opening himself, and presumably Skinner, too, to charges ranging from soft-headed oversimplification to autocratic pomposity.

Paul Goodman, an avowed utopian thinker, wrote a book called *Utopian Essays and Practical Proposals,* in which he presents his views on a wide range of practical problems of our society.[2] He says, "ideas are called utopian when they seem to be useful but they propose a different style, a different procedure, a different kind of motivation from the way people at present do business." He adds that ideas are also called utopian when "the structure and folkways of our society are absurd, but they can no longer be changed. Any hint of changing them disturbs our resignation and arouses anxiety."

Martin Buber wrote *Paths in Utopia* in 1945.[3] In it he traces historical utopian thought as a background for the experiment in Israel of the village commune of Kvuza. He explores the structure of utopianism when he says, "What, at first sight, seems common to Utopias that have passed into the spiritual history of mankind is the fact that they are pictures, and pictures, moreover, of something not actually present but only represented. . . . This 'fantasy' does not float vaguely in the air, it is not driven hither and thither by the wind of caprice, it centers with architectonic firmness on something

[1] Skinner, B. F. *Walden II*. New York: Macmillan, 1948.

[2] Goodman, P. *Utopian Essays and Practical Proposals*. New York: Random House, 1962.

[3] Buber, M. *Paths in Utopia*. Boston: Beacon Press, 1958. The 1945 edition of this book is apparently out of print.

primary and original which it is its destiny to build; and this primary thing is a wish. The utopian picture is a picture of what 'should be,' and the visionary is one who wishes it to be. . . . What is at work here is the longing for that rightness which, in idea, and which of its very nature cannot be realized in the individual, but only in human community. The vision of 'what should be'—independent though it may sometimes appear of personal will—is yet inseparable from a critical and fundamental relationship to the existing condition of humanity. . . . And what may seem impossible as a concept arouses, as an image, the might of faith, ordains purpose and plan. It does this because it is in league with powers latent in the depths of reality."

Buber blames Marx and his followers for having denounced utopian thinking, which they did from the middle nineteenth century on. He believes this isolated those socialists whose concerns included individualistic and decentralized *social* developments rather than only the centralist *economic* and *political* development favored by the Marxists. Adhering as the Marxists did to powerful centralist control and giving only lip service to the vague hope that at the propitious moment the state would wither away, Buber says they abandoned the indispensable improvisational powers of local communities and the social side of man. For the Marxists social concern and individuality were premature, therefore utopian. For them to have expected political and economic systems, built up because of immediate necessity, to commit suicide at a future propitious moment, and to give way to a socially oriented system, Buber sees as altogether unrealistic and perhaps, one might add, fraudulent, like the rabbit at the dog track. For Buber, social change need not wait for the future, but, indeed, must be an integral part of good community formation.

The Marxist split which Buber describes is also apparent in capitalist society where social needs have also taken a back seat. The varieties of social deprivation are so extensive that their existence is self-evident but the materialistic habits hang on anyway. A breakthrough in methods is needed, methods for establishing a higher priority for the fulfillment of man's social needs. Psychotherapists have found one such method for tackling the problem—the basic encounter group.

For the encounter group to have yielded this promise of swinging powerfully in rhythm with the materialistic needs which have been impelling our society, psychotherapists have had to evolve technical advances over traditional methods. These technical developments have been supported by four primary aspects of contemporary orientation, which are: (1) commonality of people problems, (2) the vectorial nature of people, (3) the characterological view, and (4) the emphasis on interactional dynamics. These considerations take priority now over the formerly preemptive importance of associational introspection, the uncovering of secrets requiring privacy, and the emphasis upon the search for the unconscious.

The first, concern with commonality of people's problems, is well illustrated by Tillich's views about existential anxiety and, later by Bugental's extension of these views. The Tillich-Bugental view is that people have four primary sources of anxiety and four consequent pathological characteristics.[4]

The sources of the underlying anxiety are Tillich's threat of death and fate, the experience of guilt and condemnation, and the confrontation with emptiness and meaninglessness. Bugental adds the threat of loneliness and isolation. The neurotic effects of these anxieties, according to Bugental, are feelings of powerlessness, blame, absurdity, and estrangement. These states are not only commonplace but universal because the rudiments of existence guarantee that we all must be confronted with these basic threats.

A further thrust giving a populist meaning to these concepts is the uncomplicated and untechnical character of the words used to designate the danger and anxiety of life. Compared to the term *castration anxiety,* for example, *powerlessness* can readily be appreciated by unsophisticated persons as immediately relevant to their lives even without expert translation. One does not need to perceive pathology in his life for these anxieties to have meaning.

[4] Bugental, J. F. T. *The Search for Authenticity.* New York: Holt, 1965; Tillich, P. *The Courage to Be.* New Haven: Yale University Press, 1952.

Powerlessness, in Bugental's terminology, is a result of man's limitations in controlling all the variables of his life. He therefore is not only ultimately challenged with death but also with a continued invitation, which he may or may not accept, to take risks. Therefore, the acceptance of the invitation to take a chance becomes a central concern in psychotherapeutic method, particularly in encounter group situations. New technologies evolve out of ideas like these, creating new social situations flowing from the developing view of man. Conceiving of man as a risk-taker rather than as a searcher into the unconscious determines new approaches and changes the entire configuration of our work as psychotherapists.

Blame is another populist concept from the Tillich-Bugental formulation. "Is this my fault?" is a question all people ask themselves. Their concern is with a possible flaw of personality which threatens their identity. Perfection may be a native goal of all people, most of us swallowing society's inculcations about what constitutes perfection and experiencing blame when we fall short of these standards. The alternative possibility is self-actualization according to one's own individual needs. In the encounter group, a part of the new technology is to foster each individual's search for his own needs in relation to the group, setting up a new relativism that freshly challenges those seeking personal fulfillment. It may be said that this has always been the intention of psychotherapy, but in my experience the search has now become more bold and adventurous than previously. It is as though we are beginning to mean what we say and experience what formerly we only hoped for.

The dread of absurdity also arises in the common view especially as the old explanations about the meaning of life, usually Judeo-Christian, become less and less convincing. Existentialism has offered a nonreligious orientation to life's nature and man's place in the world and may well be leaning to further articulations which will replace present theological systems. The new views already include the phenomenologically based efforts to recover sensory awareness, to encourage and teach bodily movement, to experience living as a present event, to know the nature of our feelings and wishes, to experience choice making, and so on. They fill the gap created by anachronistic morality and social contradictions. These and many other technical formulations of the paths to the recovery of meaning in life are being played out in the encounter movement.

The dread of apartness and estrangement accentuates the fact that we are all finite beings, unjoined to otherness yet needful of contact with otherness. The contact with others is necessary for both survival and fulfillment but is severely impeded through the many prohibitions which people experience. The encounter group is a new medium for altering morality so that people will be freed to make the necessary human contact. Touching and embracing, for example, are commonly acceptable in these groups. Expressing one's anger, boredom, confusion, excitement, love, and so on, are not necessarily evidence of boorishness, evil, ugliness, licentiousness, and so on, as they may well be under the traditional morality.

The second general aspect of contemporary orientation leading to new technical developments comes from Wilhelm Reich. Even before concern with commonality became prominent, he enunciated the importance of character analysis and led us beyond symptomatology. As is well known, the individual's everyday reactions and the details of his style of expression became central in the therapy process. Originally, Reich's interest in character came about only because he believed the removal of charcterological barriers was a prerequisite to the care of symptoms. Nevertheless, the general effect was to focus on the individual's function in everyday life. Now, we see that a person who speaks boringly rather than excitingly will diminish his sense of fulfillment. Such characteristics as tenderness, inventiveness, and fluency of language, are all viewed as central to the interactive group process and, indeed, to the individual's personal growth itself. Naturally, the importance of symptomatology is not ignored because symptoms are indeed specifically debilitating and do require attention. Furthermore, the characterology of one age may become the symptomatology of another. For example, the futility experienced by an individual whose work is inexorably wrong for him might be viewed as a symptom currently. Years ago it would not have seemed therapeutically central except as it may have led to pathology. Characterology and symptomatology are interrelated much as the melody and lyrics of a song are. Sometimes one takes precedence over the other. Nowadays the precedence of characterology plays an important technological role in permitting us an increasingly more public development of the encounter group. This is true primarily because it would seem insulting to many independently minded people to come to these groups for the cure of symptoms. The concept of the symptom reflects the isolation of a particular aspect of our lives. This has a self-depreciating effect. The individual dealing with a symptom becomes a less than global entity.

The third aspect of group process that facilitates its use in community is the view of man as having a vectorial nature. Lewin long ago described the impact of the psychological environment by proposing the concept of vectors to take account of the direction, strength, and point of application of forces affecting the individual. The concept not only described what Lewin believed important for the individual; it also served his need to make descriptive diagrams as in mathematics or physics.

Our needs currently emphasize the raw nature of one's relationship to his environment taking into account the human mechanism and its place as part of the total interplay of social forces which determine the emergence of any described event. The old forms of psychological theorizing were concerned with such factors as morality, neurosis, and the meaning of events. Naturally, we still cannot disregard such inescapable characteristics of living. Nevertheless, now there is a new appreciation of the concepts of power, giving a primary importance to managing or manipulating the power which emanates from the environment. This power threatens the individual in his innermost regions, charging him with the selection or deflection of all forces streaming into his self-experience.

Reflecting the vectorial concern are the forms of anxieties proposed by R. D. Laing.[5] These forms are engulfment, implosion, and petrifaction. Each of these, as we shall see, recognizes the power of the environment to create emphatic current effect. The concepts show appreciation of the emergency nature of ongoing events and take account of the centrality of retaining wholeness in the face of these social forces.

[5] Laing, R. D. *The Divided Self*. London: Penguin Books, 1965; and *The Self and Others*. London: Tavistock, 1961.

Engulfment, for example, is the loss of autonomy or identity through the development of relationship. One feels the risk of engulfment even when "being understood, in being loved, or even simply in being seen. To be hated may be feared for other reasons but to be hated as such is often less disturbing than to be destroyed, as it is felt, through being engulfed by love." The discovery that one may without succumbing to engulfment become understood and loved is a common phenomenon of the encounter group. The force of one's own identity remains intact even in union and in fact only through union does it become clear to the individual that his emergent nature is not a verification of his already existing identity but is a new nature currently unfolding and currently experienced. This condition creates excitement because unknown emergencies may arise at any moment and one may become newly formed before one's very own eyes and the eyes of other people with whom one is engaged.

Laing describes implosion as the filling of the individual's emptiness with new experience, "like a gas rushing in and obliterating a vacuum." People commonly resist incorporating a new experience. They have a large stake in maintaining their sensation level at an assimilable point. Each individual, knowing he can bear only a finite extent of sensation, will be wary about reaching the danger point. If one is to play life safely, one permits only the degree of sensation which stops considerably short of what is actually assimilable. Into this vacuum created by the need to stay safely away from sensation, the implosive force may enter. The individual therefore needs to discover that possible excess of sensation can be discharged, an assurance requiring an atmosphere supporting free expression. The rush, therefore, of new experience may find the individual in panic if free expression is alien to him. However, when free expression is successfully permitted, the sudden rush of crying, laughter, sexual desire, or rage will result in a new sense of completeness. Thus, the individual needs help in the encounter group in transcending his intuitive anxiety about allowing his emptiness to be filled.

Laing's third source of anxiety, petrifaction, is the process of turning a person from a living into a dead thing. The interpersonal process becomes interrupted through habits which turn away the individuality of people and the awareness of the aliveness of present experience. For example, we may categorize an individual rather than describe him. We may pretend to be interested when we are not. We may assume we know what an individual wants before it has become revealed. We may judge others by their clothes or our own needs. In reaction against these depersonalizing forces, the encounter groups become dedicated to live exchange, to discovery of the actual natures of one another, and to the recovery of the senses of autonomy and interrelatedness. To help clarify this process, the following sketch is presented. It was written following an encounter group workshop to describe the group in the process of moving from petrifaction to personal autonomy and a new community feeling.

People gather around and say we'll stay and know. But at first they do not know how for it seems like one shouldn't. It is dull to be so and each is surprised and relieved when the dullness is broken by a good word that says itself. Such a word is one which is here and says I have read Henry Miller. He says something to me and about me. But you are an assembly line inspector and stodgy and filled up too and how could you be reading so and knowing. I have to live, too, don't you know, and I don't know how out—but in there is something yet. If you can listen to it I can tell it.

I sit on my simple and play complicated. Simple is I, you, we, they, and now. It plays better than the player. It invades each heart to loosen blood and love and letting. I may. I may talk, look, listen, touch, and jump and delighted when in one sudden burst it is clear that I am here.

Here in a room with others who are all come to know what new ways there are to know and what the whole world tells of self and being. For it is especially big nowadays to *be* more—because we have done—and it is not enough.

Soon after the first surprise it is easier to talk from self and to know what sensations of self are. Work is done for this. It is embarrassing to be revealed, but hot and radiant when *they* are discovered as bending friend who receives all shock and new—without altering into gone.

The days grow and so do they into a warming *one* of trust, where all could be said and say. They soft each other into life with the flavor of new society.

The fourth factor supporting new modes of encounter is the current focus on interactional dynamics. One method representing this frame of mind is Gestalt therapy. The two primary interrelated principles which determine Gestalt therapy's view of man is that contactfulness and awareness are necessary for optimal function. Through contactfulness, man meets his environment. He confronts it and manipulates it, drawing from it that which he needs for his basic biological sustenance and for the derivative psychological necessities. As Perls, Hefferline, and Goodman have pointed out:

> Concern is felt for a present problem, and the excitement mounts toward the coming but as yet unknown solution. The assimilating of novelty occurs in the present moment as it passes into the future. Its result is never merely a rearrangement of the unfinished situations of the organism but a configuration containing a new material from the environment, and therefore different from what could be remembered (or guessed at), just as the work of an artist becomes unpredictably new to him as he handles the material medium.[6]

Given contactfulness as a guideline of human function, we might expect that group interactions would be characterized by much interpersonal confrontation. People would reach out to each other in their present situation. They would not be as likely to analyze each other's past developments as to enter into here and now statements and actions. Consequently, the creation of crises and excitement is common. The group becomes an adventure because interactional conflict replaces the older introspections *about* inner conflicts. There is a concerted effort to maximize contactfulness and to identify all possible sources of deflection from contact. The therapist must give specific attention to the characteristic ways barriers to contact are set up. He must see that certain patients look away when talking, ask questions when they mean to make statements, use lengthy introductions to simple observations, compulsively tell both sides of all stories, sit in statue-like positions, use mannerisms and expressions which reflect disinterest, play for sympathy, use submissive words when their tones are hostile, and so on, endlessly.

[6] Perls, F., Hefferline, R., and Goodman, P. *Gestalt Therapy*. New York: Dell, 1951.

These resistances are approached frontally, in the belief that with their resolution good contact will naturally follow.

Awareness which is reciprocally related to contactfulness is accentuated by phenomenological questions such as what are you feeling, what do you want, and what are you doing. These questions enable people to describe their inner process. Through this accentuation of inner process, excitement is magnified, thereby supporting the strongest interactional possibilities. Awareness is the ground upon which human existence is played out. It forms the support for contactfulness and defines the fulfillment received from the contact operations.

In the foregoing pages, the encounter group has been designated as the transitional experience moving the psychotherapy process into the community at large. In these groups many persons have learned a new depth of personal absorption through full contact with other people, through directed awareness of one's own inner process, and through experimentation with new behaviors. These are the basic ingredients of the new philosophy of encounter and the impact has revealed personal beauty too attractive to be restricted, as in the past, to people willing to be viewed as patients. Becoming aware of the half-lived life through the contrasting fuller experience of encounter group has stimulated the psychological profession to extend its hopes, leaving the private office behind and entering into new fellowship and mutuality with people who are in their accustomed haunts and who are carrying on their familiar functions. The flower is wild and must be appreciated where it lives.

Before proceeding to a description of community exploration, we will now touch base about our readiness for a social psychotherapy, where some of its antecedents are and what the implications are for life in our society.

Many years ago during a discussion with the clergy about the commonalities and differences between psychotherapy and religion, I said teasingly that one of the main differences between the two was that psychotherapists try to put themselves out of business whereas religionists are self-perpetuating. Though I preferred the psychotherapists' attitude at the time, I later came to realize that we have been deluding ourselves through the concept of terminated therapy. We have hoped, if not expected, that after working privately with people for six months or six years, a terminal moment will come and our services will no longer be needed. That this hope is fruitless is now abundantly clear. The expectation of global resolutions ignores the fact that life's most problematic engagements occur repeatedly and we can expect never to be rid of them. Problems centering around death, birth, marriage, loss of job, exclusion from one community or another, expression of self, misunderstandings, new ventures, and so on, are the core of ongoing lives and thus far we as psychotherapists have had no constituted continuity in our relationships with people who live such lives.

The people of religion do involve themselves in these inexorable aspects of living. But they have been operating with severe theological and institutional handicaps and frequently look to the psychological fields to fill the gaps in personal experience fostered by their system. The priority posed in the relationship of man to God has overshadowed the contact between man and man. Psychotherapists have been filling this breach especially recently, by their insights concerning the impactfulness of the encounter. We have known since Freud about the special, even volatile, powers which exist in the psychotherapy encounter. Breuer was frightened when he discovered the intensity of the feelings that his patients developed for him. Freud's discovery of transference acknowledged this intensity. Through this concept, the therapist for many years was able to keep his distance from the fullest potency which developed through the condensed power of the psychotherapy encounter. Over the years we have been learning to accept the intensity of this encounter at its face value. We are now closer to treating it as an authentic interaction revealing the nature of all the people engaged whether in private therapy or in a group situation. The widespread habits of deflection and depersonalization, which have evolved through proliferated politeness, structured grammar, and avoidance of the natural flow of one's own mind, have stored up large quantities of energy. When somebody tells a real truth that is meaningful, pointed, and previously blocked, a room of people becomes enlivened and very deeply absorbed. Because of the extensions in time spent together, there are new opportunities to resolve unfinished situations. This potentiality is increased even though the group impactfulness sometimes comes too fast, even though there may be excessive and unassimilable energy released, and even though the complications of personal interaction may require sorting and interweaving. The power of these experiences may arise through provocative, brash or hurting interactions, or the power may come when a well-timed statement genuinely touches a person. A simple remark like "I think you are a very sensitive man" may bring on tears from a man who has never before been viewed as sensitive. A touch of the hand may bespeak profound acceptance.

With such a power as is inherent in encounter groups, it is only a short step to go beyond the retreat situation into those which normally exist all around us. We already have used encounter methods as a new approach to old consulting requirements. This includes working with education systems, including teachers, administrators, and pupils; industrial executives; religious enclaves and church groups; Synanon; staff development programs; workshops for lay persons; workshops for therapists; and, of course, all this in addition to the expanding use of group therapy methods in working with classical patients. Now we are also becoming emboldened to explore in uncharted community settings where psychotherapists have not only had little prior experience, but deep resistance to participation.

One example, among a growing number of them, is my exploration of psychotherapy methods in a public coffee house. A series of coffee house meetings called Encounter was arranged. The meetings were conducted from the stage at regular coffee house evening hours as a part of the public and semicommercial aspect of the enterprise. This particular coffee house was deep in the heart of a Cleveland hippie land. The coffee house was under repeated harassment by the police, partly because of their concern with the possible drug traffic and partly because of supposed disturbances which the coffee house aroused in the neighborhood. We met irregularly, averaging about once every two weeks from July 1967 to March 1968, when the coffee house was destroyed by fire.

These coffee house sessions were set up to explore the encounter possibilities in large community settings. Three main purposes formed the foundation of our engagement. The first was to activate group participation to dramatize the underlying modes of experience that existed in the community. The second was to establish the validity of topic-centeredness within the encounter or therapeutic process. The third was to permit and encourage changes in the attitudes or self-experiences where these were self-defeating.

The first purpose, the activation of group participation, was an attempt to counteract the familiar spectator character of most large group situations. The outsize demands of talking to a crowd of lined-up strangers are familiarly torturous. Large audiences, though they promise magnified liveliness, can also be unmanageably depersonalized. In the art of public communication only the best of us can retain feelings of immediacy or personal effect. The unilateral statement reigns in religion, politics, education, entertainment, and advertising. Little room exists for the working-through process. Religious services are often so stereotyped, repetitive, and irrelevant that one rabbi was able to tell me, half in humor and half in dismay, that some of his most knowledgeable people make excuses to him for having come to the services. One person explains to him that his child happened to be singing in the chorus; another explains he is only interested in a certain speaker; another comes for some special commemorative experience. In politics, strategy transcends all questions of sincerity or immediacy.

Can the encounter group style be assimilated into large groups or even conferences? In the encounter group we learn personal interaction by splitting into smallnesses, no larger a group than would permit everybody the chance to unfold in a way that is personally appreciated. Undoubtedly these opportunities represent a large advance; not so great an advance as to create all we need. The small group is too small a world to live in. In society, since interconnectedness and interdependence are unavoidable, there must be some way of relating to the larger community. Otherwise we invite secrecy, which does characterize current psychotherapy practices, or we become esoteric, spreading bewilderment when we approach the uninitiated. In experiencing the largeness of the community, there is a contagion of spirit which stretches beyond the exclusive workings of the now familiar intimate smallness of the encounter group. We have much to learn about meeting in mass but it is clear that the harmonious presence of many people magnifies our own inner experience and our relatedness to others. This challenge is relevant now wherever responsiveness is minimal.

In the coffee house, conversation and play were the common mode among the customers. That was what they came for. Nevertheless, they needed some activities which could bring the total group together. Usually this would happen through poetry readings, musical performances, and even lectures. These were the only ways they did come together as a united group. The spontaneity of their ordinary dialogue would be interrupted by these spectator experiences. Our wish was to bring the total room together by including spontaneous interaction. Naturally our possibilities were limited by the deliberateness required in starting the encounter session. The proprietor would get on the stage to introduce me and I would explain what we were trying to do. People were permitted to come and go as they pleased or to talk to each other or not. The customers would be different from meeting to meeting, though a core of people would come repeatedly. Naturally, certain disadvantages existed, such as lack of follow-through with people who did not come repeatedly. Some people would leave before resolutions could be reached, but the advantage we gained was that we stayed closer to the real community by making only minimal restrictions and arrangements.

Our first meeting was centered around the topic of hippies and a policeman and illustrates the participating body which emerged in these sessions. People were selected to role-play a hippie and a policeman in conversation. They started out saying very stereotyped words to each other. The policeman wanted the hippie to go out and get a job, quit wearing crazy hairdos and clean up. He described the hippie as being unruly, dangerous, and unappetizing. The hippie, on the other hand, saw the policeman as a brute—cold, lacking understanding, insensitive, unreachable. At first no matter what I would say to them the responses remained stereotyped and cruel. When confronted with outlandishness of some of his remarks, the policeman at one point was taken aback and began to examine his feelings. He then said that he really had a job to do and could not afford to have much feeling about what he was doing. He just wanted to get it over with. He did not want to have to think about it. Furthermore, he was afraid he might get hurt if he did not stay tough. The hippie did not give any specific recognition to the change in tone of the policeman and continued talking as he had before. When this was called to his attention he recognized that this was true. He recognized that it might now be possible to communicate with the policeman. But he said he did not want to. He wanted the policeman to remain an impossible person against whom he could vent his anger and his superiority. He wanted to continue to be angry and if he could possibly avoid recognizing and accepting the fact that the policeman was different, he would do so. Thus he continued to be adamant and vocal even arousing cheers from the audience when he would get off an especially eloquent line. He was unwittingly making a very important commentary on the nature of conflict, even as it relates to the large social movements, such as black-white confrontation and conflicts between nations. A great force of unexpressed and unsatisfied inner experience builds up and must have its opportunity to emerge. When conditions against which these experiences are directed change and when the expression of inner experience has not been completed, the need to complete the blocked expression remains. One is likely, therefore, to ignore changes in the environment until one's need is completed. The militant blacks have unfinished business and have to release their fury as though no improvements have developed. The variations in timeliness among parties to a conflict cause considerable trouble. One side is resolved, the other is not. Thus, by reacting as though the old conditions were still true, resolutions must be delayed until the party with unfinished business can complete his accumulated need for expression.

In this coffee house session there were about 125 people present. Unlike the ordinary audience, this one actively participated. People began to question the right of the policeman to say that which they felt had no foundation in reality and which they felt illustrated not only his errors of thinking but was also symbolic of the errors in the thinking of society as a whole. As the situation developed, the policeman and the hippie were asked to switch roles.

They did this much to the relief of the man who had been playing the policeman. He now suddenly became quite relaxed in the friendly atmosphere. The switch in roles aroused the audience to the dynamics of role-playing and the implications of the barrier-free situation. They also wanted to play roles and several groups of persons did. Soon a communal spirit had developed. There was considerable communication similar to the type one might find in a very large therapy situation. Then, the last person to play the role of the policeman left the stage and went to the rear of the room to arrest the proprietor, confronting him with certain violations which would make him subject to arrest. The proprietor refused to give the policeman full information, standing on his rights to give only his full name. The policeman then told the proprietor that he was under arrest and proceeded to lead him to the door of the coffee house. The proprietor did not go willingly but resisted only a little as he respected and feared the power of the policeman. The people in the audience, however, began to shout "don't let him take him away," leaving their tables to join in a rescue attempt. A wild melee ensued. People were swinging their arms, lifting chairs threateningly, shouting. Anyone entering the coffee house at that moment would have felt certain that a riot was in progress. When the force of their aggression had spent itself and the rescue operation had succeeded, the people returned to their tables. They had a feeling of having yielded to a powerful drama. What had begun as simple role playing by two people had ended as a most dramatic audience role-playing situation. The community involvement gave a cathartic and poetic line to the expression of 125 people. When all became seated again, there was an air of hushed awe at what had happened. A large group had walked the line between poetry and the reality. Though one could not always tell the difference between the poetry and the reality the individuals in the group, though fully invested, were aware of their perspective and never allowed the dramatic situation to carry them into acts which would have been disharmonious with the existing conditions. Nobody used the situation as an excuse for actual violence. The group discussed the meaning of the experience and the prevailing view was that people were expressing their suppressed aggression against the police—acting out in the role-playing situation what they would like to do in real life, but have felt powerless. This powerlessness resulted, said they, in their feeling of alienation and, furthermore, the opportunity to act the scene out brought them together into a sense of community.

Another illustration of extensive audience involvement was an encounter session on riots and hostility. The topic had been suggested the previous week by the audience and the enthusiasm for it was great. The audience was packed, standing five deep around the room of filled tables. Three people were selected to play roles; one was to play a conservative, another apathy, and the other a Black Muslim. Immediately after the role playing began it became evident that the conservative was playing an extremist role. He was extremely derisive about Negroes. He flung invective about their dirtiness, their animal natures, and their repulsiveness. He accused them of having garbage cans for back yards, of being stupid, lazy, and stinking. He was very pervasively vituperative and insulting. The reaction was very powerful. One Negro rushed up from the back of the room, shouting furiously at the conservative, responding not as a spector of a stage drama, but as though this invective had been aimed directly at him. Here again it would have been difficult to know whether this was reality or poetry. The atmosphere was electric. It was profoundly absorbing, frightening, and surprising to be sitting in a room where violence could erupt at any moment, yet there was, nevertheless, considerable trust that this would not happen. Indeed, the most volatile of the black people climbed the stage at the end of the session to tell the audience that he loved them despite the anger-making scene. I tried working with the conservative to determine how he felt about getting the kind of reactions he was getting. He became quite confused for a moment because he did not know whether I wanted him to continue role playing or whether he was to tell what his own true feelings were. I asked him to continue role playing but to also tell how he felt and to allow himself the freedom to play the role any way he wanted to. He immediately returned to the original adamant vituperative position, expressing none of his personal reactions to the verbal onslaught which his words had brought on. It became apparent that he was completely inflexible as long as he was playing a role. I ex-

plained this process to the audience and to him, the process wherein
the people who play roles in the society have lost their freedom,
their individuality, and their openness to experiencing the present
moment. They wind up with stereotyped, programmed living, experiencing little free choice. This was a dramatic illumination to
them. At the next session we continued the same topic but changed
the role-playing scene. The audience became very active, many
people again presenting their views about racial questions. At one
point a young girl called out from the rear of the room, confronting
a man playing a liberal suburbanite with his backward ideas. She
entered into a heated exchange with him. He asked her whether
she would date a Negro bay and she said of course she would. She
then went on to describe her happy relationships with Negro boys,
seeming quite unself-conscious, unapologetic, and dramatically simple
in her statements of freedom of choice irrespective of race. The feeling in the room grew into a feeling of unity and many people
described their feelings about race relations. The issue of black
power arose. Considerable support for black power was voiced,
especially among the Negroes. A climactic moment arrived when a
young white man arose and expressed his fury at the black power
people because of having been turned away by a Negro group at
the anti-Vietnam war demonstrators in New York City. He had
come there to join in the march and had wanted to enter with a
group of Negroes. They told him they didn't want to have any
white man joining them. Thus, he poured out his frustration. The
tension in the room grew. Then, after several exchanges, one of the
black power adherents stood up on his chair and with what I felt
as touching eloquence, tenderly spoke to this man in the crowded
audience telling him about the Negro's needs for identification and
for self-propulsion. He said that they hoped white men would take
a path parallel to their own and that they could join together again
later. In the meantime, he wanted this man to be patient and
recognize the Negro's need for establishing his own identity without
white support. The statement had an electric quality. The dangers
of violence or vituperation were so great that the contrast created
by this man's tenderness and articulateness were a great relief and

offered so renewed a perspective on the problem that the audience rested and the session ended.

The second of our purposes was to include topic-centeredness in the encounter situation. Topic-centeredness is frequently excluded from group therapy situations, which focus upon personal experience of the participants and frown upon intellectualism. In some of my therapy groups when an individual brings up topics like the Vietnam war, contemporary architecture, the political structure, current events, teaching techniques, and so on, many people in the groups will protest that these issues are not relevant to their own personal explorations. Actually, nothing is further from the truth. Our lives are tied into external events. As long as we do not depersonalize, we must unite our interests with those of the environmental forces. Indeed, when we have in these groups been able to join personal feeling with discussions of environmental conditions such as the Vietnam war, powerful interactions have developed. One man, after a lengthy discussion of the Vietnam war, said his son might be getting into it and gave his own impassioned view of the conflict, developing real grief about the many deaths and his own deeply felt terror about his son entering it. Psychotherapists, through our theories of personal introspection and our concern with only what is immediately before us, may, in developing group psychotherapy, have cut out the substance of our existences and made our group situations overly stylized and irrelevant. In these coffee house sessions, we have tried to move beyond these limitations and have tried to develop topics as a core around which the encounters emerge. The previous illustrations, though centered around topics, had their most powerful effect as audience dramas. The next illustrations, however, although also involving audience participation, reveal the importance of topic-centeredness in the community encounter. The topic was hippies and straight people.

Arrangements had been made for a group of so-called straight people to attend our session. These people served at another Cleveland coffee house. They were friendly with hippies and respectful but lived well-organized lives, dressed conventionally, lived in familiar family relationships, and worked in continuing jobs. In addition to the invited straight people there were others who just came in. Thus, there were at least as many so-called straight people as there were so-called hippies.

The session started out stiffly but it was not long before one of the hippies confronted the straight people by brazenly accusing them of unwillingness to participate actively. His name was Jack and he became the center of a storm. He was experienced as shoving his stereotypes down the throats of the people present. The straight people did not like it but they were at a disadvantage because they were accustomed to politeness and permissiveness and they were taken aback by the sudden and stark attack. The ball was rolling, though, and a marked polarization developed between the so-called hippies and the so-called straight people. Each side was unhappy to categorize and did not like being called either hippy or straight. The idea that all people are individual and ought to be treated as such was predominant. Nevertheless, in spite of these high-minded attitudes, each side was considerably stereotyped about the other and became very defensive about its own position. Some of the straight people finally became so angry that they left their seats and walked toward Jack and some of the other hippies haranguing them about their refusal to examine them as individual people. They said Jack and his associates were presumptuous. The straight people were especially irate when Jack accused them of coming down to the coffee house to get respite from their dreary lives. Other statements were equally confronting. In the beginning there was little effort to find out about other people's lives. Everybody seemed to know. As the session continued, people within the hippie group began to speak out against Jack's view and to point out that they really cared about the straight people. They did want to make contact on an individual and respectful basis. One hippie girl said they were afraid of the straight people because they were older and because they were really afraid of their own parents. They would like to join their parents but knew they could not. She said her own father would never be caught dead in a place like the coffee house and always refused to have anything to do with her views concerning life. She was glad the straight people had come. This view was echoed by others. They wanted an expansion of their community and an expansion of their opportunity for communicating with people who have made it in society. One girl thought that in hearing the views expressed that the straight people were nothing but old hippies.

The concept of topic-centeredness pervaded all of our sessions just as did the concept of audience participation and drama. A list of the topics includes psychedelic trips, how to experience change, how to create change, hippies and teachers, hippies and schools, sex between the races, how to evade the draft, the meaning of war, getting along without money, the relationship of love and sex, the needs of the coffee house community, hippies and policemen, hippies and straight people, riots and hostility, religion and society, and listening and communication. All of these topics aroused very lively interactions. Frequently these interactions were verbally aggressive. Aggressiveness and directness would almost invariably turn the session into an exciting one. Intellectual discussions invariably toned the room down and resulted in impatience and restlessness. The statement which strongly affected another individual person was the one most likely to pay off in good communication and a sense of unified community.

The third condition underlying our coffee house sessions was the effort to work through problems characteristically experienced by members of the group. One of our sessions dealt with the coffee house people's hang-ups about communicating to people outside of their small groups. There had been a vigorous encounter two weeks earlier about religion. There had been quite a few religionists in the coffee house; some were from an urban ministry program, another group were evangelists who had been asked to come for this night. I introduced the evening by saying we would continue with the topic of religion as we had not finished it the previous time. One of the hippies immediately said that he did not believe in God, thereby dismissing religion altogether. He felt, as I pointed out to him, that God and religion were indispensable to each other and that there was no way to talk about one without talking about the other. He thought it was all a great hoax set up to make people do things they did not want to do and he wanted no part of it. There were echoes of similar sentiment from others in the room. Most of it was deflected and mumbled with an impatience suggesting there really was not much to talk about. Some thoughts about religion were developed which went beyond God and into personal desires, meaningfulness, and so on. One person said his own religion was based on morality rather than God, and that his morality was a morality of self. He said that when he felt that he was doing something "correctly" that he was being moral and religious. This, he believed, had nothing to do with God or the conventional principles of morality. I asked him when he experienced himself doing things correctly, therefore realizing his own religious directions. He said he was doing things correctly right now. As he said this his face rose in a lovely smile, his radiance giving evidence that he did indeed feel that what he was saying was correct and that for him this was an authentically religious experience. In the meantime, one table of about ten hippies was noisy and unwilling to be fully involved in the proceedings. Every once in a while they would engage in perceptive catcalling, making some diminishing remarks about religion but not really engaging with the rest of the room. I became interested in this group. Without their participation it seemed like the discussion would be limited. Furthermore, they were the very people for whom the discussions were intended. Therefore, it was necessary to face up to their disinterest and restlessness.

It was not long before people in the room were beginning to be annoyed with these people. One woman finally arose, loudly remonstrating with them for their refusal to be reached and for their discourtesy. She also wanted to be heard by them. One of them said she was being belligerent and that they did not dig belligerence. The question arose as to whether they would listen to ordinary communication or whether they would respond only to excessive energy.

One man said that these young people had something very special among themselves, great mutual acceptance and deep enjoyment which he felt was a religious expression. Another minister at the other end of the room said he did not think this was very religious at all. He said they were nothing more than a clique refusing to engage with others in society.

After considerable discussion, one of the hippies got up and said, addressing the room in general, "Make it, don't fake it." He said most of the people in the room were not honest and there was no way to have any good communication if people were being phony. This aroused a mountainous rage in me which poured out from the frustrations in communication. I confronted these people with the realities of good communication and the difficulties in communicating beyond one's own restricted clique. They were taking very little responsibility for good contact and I resented their closed system, which threw out potshots every now and then about the worthlessness of whatever did not crack into their system. I left the stage and approached them screaming my words. They now began to listen to my impassioned words about their clique which judges others without listening. When I was done they said to me, "We are not interested in talking about religion, we want to talk about riots." Finally they had said what they were really interested in. Immediately, the room came alive. Somebody referred to whites as honkies. Feelings became aroused and what followed was a familiar encounter session phenomenon of powerful assertiveness in a nonviolent context. This is refreshing because it permits aggressive expression without the usual risks. As we went on the group became more nearly unified than before; not unified in agreement but unified in personal involvement.

XI

Intensity in Group Encounter

John Warkentin

The danger common to all psychotherapeutic methods is lack of sufficient involvement by the participants. This is particularly true with groups. When I began group work some twenty-five years ago, I did it in order to make therapy less expensive to patients and to enable me to treat more people. I soon learned that these were false bases. In recent years, by contrast, I have learned to recommend group therapy as the most effective and challenging kind of growth effort I can make available.

The problem is how to achieve enough intensity. Psychological healing efforts since the early nineteen hundreds have involved many different techniques, systems of thought, and schools of treatment in order to achieve sufficient impact on psychological patients to result in healing or growth. However, from the Freudian couch to the nude therapies of today (dry or wet) there has never been devised a technique or system that will get people well. There are no tricks of our trade that help us to mature. This is true for any patient where character change is intended, but is particularly obvious in group patients. The various techniques employed by therapists are useful in bringing people into apposition, but no more. Thereafter the outcome depends on the person's continuing involvement. The techniques we use can make it easier for persons to begin a relationship. If a sustained effort in relating is to follow, the results will depend on what might be called the person factor in therapy. This factor is really an equation, in which the nature of the therapist plus the motivation of the patient results in healing and growth.

The therapists who find group work most successful are those whose personal presentation and character structure lead them into intense relating with several people simultaneously. They have developed a conviction arising out of their own emotional growth efforts that most (if not all) adults harbor a profound drive to continue growing. Effective group therapists do not expect this drive to be manifested in their patients as if by spontaneous combustion. They are prepared to employ opener techniques, and to risk involving their own persons. The effective group therapist is the first to expose himself to the mercy of the group. There may be times when the therapist sits out a delay in group participation, but more often he is likely to be ready to enliven the group experience by means of personal questions, suggestions to participants which will relieve them of some ambivalence, or personal comments about group members. In all of this he is careful to maintain a group focus, which means strict avoidance of his doing individual therapy on just one participant at a time. Such individual therapy in the group constitutes subgrouping, which reduces intense group interaction just as much as if the subgrouping were a private conversation between some other two participants.

The value of techniques to a group, such as holding hands, I explain as temporary pump-priming. In trying to explain the necessity of a sustained active relating between all members of the group I may mention that there could have been no emotional growth possible for Robinson Crusoe on his deserted island unless his man Friday had arrived. I usually encourage participants to think about their group effort for at least an hour or two before each session, to avoid alcoholic drinks then, and to plan to extend the expression of their person beyond whatever limits they had in the previous session. This has the effect of greatly increasing group anxiety without causing the group to sit in frozen silent tension. I remind participants that feelings are mutual, that my group therapy sessions are the most anxious hours of my work week, and that they are therefore my most valued hours. The therapist's person factor is particularly important in the early sessions of a new group, before the group can devise techniques to immobilize themselves. However, I also explain that all close human relationships seem to drift toward lesser and lesser involvement until the relationship seems impassed, unless all of us participants actively relight the fires of our anxieties periodically.

The second person factor is the motivation of the patients. In order to achieve any significant change in ourselves it is necessary to make a commitment to seek very active and close relatedness to the other participants. For example, as long as a married couple are determined to love only each other it would not be appropriate to refer them to the kind of group work I am discussing. Their motivation needs to be consciously clear, that the participants will not hide from other group members in any way, and that the participants feel a readiness for increasingly intense group related-ness.

Usually I see a person or married couple in office visits for some time before asking, "Have you thought of promoting your growth effort in group therapy?" Depending on the psychological sophistication of the person, they may reply, "Yes, I'd heard that you want all your patients to join a group, but I just don't think I'm ready to spill my guts in public." Another reply might be, "Yes, I know groups have a lot to offer me, but I'm not even related enough to you as yet, leave alone to take on a whole bunch of people." Such objections indicate the person's distrust of multiple human involvement and his ignorance of the opportunities available only in groups. I am likely to let the matter rest for the time being with a comment such as, "Let's keep the question open between us, and you can let me know when you want to hear a taped discussion or two regarding group therapy (between appointments, without charge); you can also ask me for a memo about some details regarding group therapy whenever you are ready." Subsequently, when the person is ready to consider group participation again, I usually also offer him some reading matter on the subject, to give him some feeling about the possibilities of group success and failure.

Such gradual referral to a group may well take many months. A person seems ready to make the most of a group opportunity when he is prepared to commit himself to participate freely regarding all aspects of his past and present living. He is then ready to accept whatever anxieties and tensions it may cost him, with a promise to himself and to me that he will be physically present if at all possible for every meeting of the group for a given number of months. With the inward and outward agreement to participate with others on whatever the emotional wavelength may be, he has set the stage to move toward intimate encounters with every member of the group. Such movement of the participants toward each other, with increasing intensity, must not be limited to any one feeling tone or wavelength. Intense closeness may be experienced with the feeling of anger, jealousy, fear, sexuality, affection, and so on, and any modality must be acceptable to the therapist. If the therapist places any restrictions on the human interactions in a group this immediately limits the possibilities for intense encountering and can even reduce the group to social chit-chat as the prevailing mode of interaction. For example, if the therapist prohibits personal indifference between group members, this is just as much a hindrance as if he were to prohibit expressions of hatred or some other particular feeling experience.

The dominance of the therapist results from his nature, not from details of his behavior. His personal readiness to be an active participant will set the tone of the group in its early meetings, and his inner dynamics will continue to dominate the group, no matter how he may give expression to his thoughts and feelings. For ex-

ample, whenever I sit down with a new group it is with the purpose
that I might learn a greater respect and affection for each member
of the group in the months to come. As a result, the usual experience in my groups is that participants discover increasing affection
for each other. Where two people experience a rather prompt dislike for each other in the early sessions, I am likely to suggest that
they keep sitting next to each other and try to touch each other as
much as possible until they get better acquainted.

Another example of how I dominate the dynamics of a new
group is as follows: A professional man about my own age sat in
silence during the first half of the first meeting, obviously becoming
irritated, until he blurted out, "John, I thought you were supposed
to be a skilled group therapist, and we are just having a messy
mish-mash. I've never been in a group before, but I could run it
better than this." I replied, "How could we get under way more
effectively?" The group was tense and silent as he thought for a
moment and then said, "Well, I could ask some leading questions
so that each one of us at least got involved, and I'm used to being
a leader." I agreed, "Sounds good, lead off." He then went from
person to person around the group, having memorized their first
names during the initial introduction. He asked why they were
seeking treatment, whether they hoped to get any, and he used the
rest of the group period in this way. When one of the other participants turned to me and asked, "Are you going to let him run this
thing?" I just shrugged my shoulders and put up my hands in a
gesture of helplessness. Barely before the time was up, our self-
elected leader said, with a new tension in his voice, "I forgot to tell
you why I'm here. My problem is that I can't relax, I can't stop
being a leader, I don't know how to be just one of the people." The
group had not been hostile to him, although one of the women
made some mildly sarcastic comments (she "enjoyed him because
he was funny"). In subsequent meetings he learned to listen, much
to his wife's surprise. More than other members, he had acted out
a very troublesome part of his living in that first session; my leadership was thereafter assured, and the group became a particularly
meaningful and intense experience for him as he dared gradually to
let us in on his fearfulness and tenderness.

Not only the therapist's maturity but also his open verbal participation influences the entire group process. After several months of group effort, a young woman with a repressive background became openly resentful that she was being criticized frequently for her prudishness. She had shared much of her feeling and history, but omitted sexual details all along. When she modestly and repeatedly pulled her skirt down, another participant began suggesting routinely, "Now pull it back up," but she never did this. She had made some comments on occasion that everybody had their own feet of clay, even the great psychiatrist. After further provocation in one session, she said with agitation and anger, "O.K., John, how often do *you* masturbate?" I answered her honestly, feeling her hidden fear beneath the angry exterior. There was a shocked silence in the room. Her eyes softened, and for the rest of the period she shared with us a flood of emotionally loaded experiences regarding such details of her early life as her seductive father. This seemed to constitute a significant turning point in her life-orientation, and the beginning of a delightful softening of her previously rigid person. It was also a new start for the whole group because they now included me as a regular participant as never before. Some weeks later, two other members took me to task because my wife had been seriously ill and I had not brought this to the group. They felt that they had been deprived of sharing in my hurt and depression, and felt that I should have volunteered to speak of my own struggles just as they did. I agreed to this. In this group and in others I saw it as a special privilege that I could participate also as the unadorned human animal.

It is an advantage to the group therapist when his anxiety and tension are readily apparent. Sweating palms and armpits, trembling, irregular breathing, restlessness, flushing of the face, all these and other symptoms of emotional stress in the therapist assure the other participants that feelings are really mutual. In addition, it is a learning at gut level for the entire group to discover that great anxiety can bring people together in more intense relatedness. Repeatedly participants will conclude after the final ending of a group that one of their major new strengths is the discovery that anxiety is like "gas in the tank." In addition, it is rare for anyone to go through such experiences without learning that human intimacy is always preceded by much fearfulness.

No ground rules are necessary in the kind of group where participants are committed to a growth effort. In my early years as group therapist I tried to work out rules which would facilitate group interaction, but now I see these merely as suggestions which the other participants may choose to "disobey." I still say "the only rule is that we have no physical violence." However, this has never been an issue anyway in adult groups of people making a serious effort with each other. I do make many suggestions as we go along, offer many rules of thumb, and teach as much as seems appropriate from time to time regarding ways in which human nature seems to work best, and other ways which do not work. Some of my suggestions to a new group follow.

Confidentiality is necessary for group freedom of expression. I suggest that the participants not mention even to their closest friends that they are making a growth effort, or give the name of the leader, times of meetings, or other information. I suggest that we use only first names in the group, and that we otherwise maintain social anonymity as far as possible.

Stopping the group discussion at the end of each session serves the useful purpose of promoting further inner consideration of the questions raised in each participant. Even where husband and wife are both in the same group, I suggest that they speak of other things when they leave. I suggest that group members not socialize together at any time outside the group meeting, lest their social contacts water down the intense impact on each other in the setting where no holds are barred.

Resistance to intimacy is so great in all of us that I suggest techniques to overcome it. As a symbol of our freedom with each other, I suggest that we take off our shoes for the sessions, and that each person try to remain in physical contact with his neighbors on each side, which requires sitting quite closely together. In regard to content, I repeatedly mention that we should bring our most troublesome or embarrassing thoughts and feelings out into the open at the very beginning of each session, so that we will have time to live together around the issues raised. I suggest that all adults must normally live with many secrets, but that the group is a place for abnormal openness regarding all the secrets of our lives, so that we may know forever that there is no part of our experience which other human beings cannot share with us.

Learning to listen carefully may be even more difficult to achieve than learning to speak openly. Sometimes even five minutes of absolute silence in a group may develop enough anxiety in some of us to take a new step in our relatedness to others. This learning-to-be-silent also is necessary so that the group will allow enough room to a person who introduces a significant struggle, so that the group effort is focused on the matter until it comes to some conclusion; otherwise the group may continuously "spider" its effort in all directions at once, or skip around in such quick succession that it is not meaningful to anybody.

Administrative details must be clear. The therapist is responsible for selecting group participants, in such a way that they have a readiness to make use of the group opportunity. It helps if the group members are in the same general age bracket, and sufficiently close to each other in socioeconomic status to speak the same language. Closed groups develop a more lively interaction, and I would not even bring in a guest therapist without first clearing this with the group, usually some time in advance. The financial relationship between therapist and other participants needs to be clear, with no members in arrears on payment, lest this create an extraneous hindrance to free movement. The dates of beginning and ending of the group need to be clear so that we can all make an inner adjustment or establish an unconscious set in relationship to the time elements. Periodically I also offer much longer sessions than the usual one-and-a-half hours or two-and-a-half hours of regular meetings. These longer marathon meetings are open only to people who are working with me in groups. These run for twenty hours, which appears to be the usual limit of our anxiety span. These marathons are times of major effort to get past some issues which were not possible to deal with in the shorter sessions. Just as in the short sessions, I suggest that people come prepared to deal with their most troublesome concerns as early as possible in the marathon session, lest they be tempted to sit it out because others have more important issues to present. It has seemed helpful in marathons for people to make every effort to stay wide awake, to move about the room periodically, change seats during the session, and otherwise keep both their bodies and their spirits as lively as possible. A final detail pertaining to marital partners is my suggestion that they prepare to be present as if they were single during the session, that they not sit with each other, and that they not protect or criticize each other.

The group process is often unclear to me. The multitude of interacting lines of communication between us nine or ten people in a group are so many, the feelings are often too hidden from my grasp, so that I simply give up trying to "understand" in the way that I do in office visits. I do try to register on the major sweeps and waves of feeling and intense interaction, how they build up, what breakthrough may occur, and how these waves of movement alternate with other periods of relative inactivity or even indifference. The periods of low feeling activity often seem ideal for some further installments of teaching, spelling out some paradoxes in human nature, the peculiar differences between us, and the tremendous similarity among all human beings.

The group farewell is worth doing well. My closed groups may meet for four months, six months, or a year, and in one instance the same four married couples constituted a group for three years. Whatever the calendar time involved, the participants are likely to have met each other as persons so significantly that their separation should be undertaken even more thoughtfully than was their initial coming together. I try to facilitate the gradual farewell by mentioning occasionally how many more sessions we have left, and particularly to emphasize my hope that none of the group will leave prematurely in the face of the approaching separation anxiety. They may have met as fortunate strangers, but they are likely to be separating as significant others.

XII

Tradition Innovation

Stewart B. Shapiro

The principles of encountering find special meaning for certain professional groups who by convention and position lose the intimate human touch even though their specific function may be human affairs. One such group is the Church Executive Development Board of the National Council of Churches. This paper involves a discussion of a one-week residential encounter program in which a special form, tradition innovation, was used to implement a rediscovery of feeling and affect, and improve human relations generally. While bishops, administrative officers of synods and dioceses, directors of finance, district Sunday School directors, and similar others made up the encounter groups, the theory and methodology employed with them has application to other groups as well. Most of the participants were over the age of forty, and many were in their fifties or sixties.

My colleagues and I formulated general goals based on what we knew about the men and women participating, their backgrounds, needs, and expectations. (In each group, there were one or two women executives, which I feel further added to the experience.) Our goals were:

We wanted to help them experience a wide range of affect, anger, strength, anxiety, love, tenderness, power, sadness, and so on. We are particularly interested in helping them to accept their angry, hostile feelings and to develop constructive ways for them to express negative affect. These were people, we felt, who had the most difficulty with hostility. They tended to deny it whether it was directed toward them or experienced by them. They had very few constructive models for the expression of aggression—and it caused them all kinds of difficulties in both their professional and personal lives.

We wanted to encourage them in the congruent use of influence. These were men and women of great responsibility and often of great potential power. Many of them abhorred the idea of power and influence, having been reared in deeply religious Christian backgrounds—where especially the direct use of power or manipulation was often considered sinful. Even if they had been blood-and-thunder fundamentalists in the past, most of them hesitated now to be aggressive, and all too frequently their current leadership situations begged for direct, decisive action. In short, we regarded them as "power-shy."

We hoped that they would be able to make some kind of statement of their personal goals through the group interaction. We wanted them to try to relate these personal goals to their organizational goals—to integrate their needs wherever possible (for example, personal preference for ecumenism versus a church essentially fighting against it).

We wanted them to become more aware of their role conflicts and to help them deal synergestically with these conflicts. We believed that they experienced role and value conflicts which other executives did not face to the same degree. These include the professed, idealized, personal Christian goals versus contradictory, realistic, day-to-day demands—or behavior unbecoming a "true

Christian." For example, they had difficulty with competition although many of them and their organizations were in highly competitive situations. Another conflict was their feeling for tradition and high value placed on the reactive side of their organizations, as opposed to the modern demands on the church for rapid change and innovation. Another conflict was their original ministerial or pastoral functioning as opposed to their current function as administrators. Formerly they ministered directly to people; now they worked with papers, numbers, boards, and the like. Their previous idealized image of themselves was prophetic, with no conscious strategy, or direct power, and perhaps an eventual martyrdom. Their jobs now often desperately called for the effective use of power.

We wanted to help them integrate and extend their ability to experience positive feelings like joy, love, strength, and serenity. Our lab was to have an underlying "positive thrust," and this is where I came in.[1]

I first introduced the concept of tradition innovation in a prospectus for a cross-cultural anthropology laboratory at the UCLA Institute of Industrial Relations in April, 1966, and developed it further in a paper.[2] The basic idea is to use the phenomenon of culture shock positively; "To study and experience cultures other than our own, primitive or modern, and to come up with new traditions, customs, or rituals which could be incorporated into Western tradition. We are seeking traditions that 'make sense'; possibly the development of a new local language, new symbols, new folklore, and a new mythology. The 'new culture,' to be sure, might be composed of a mixture of old, forgotten traditions in our own Western civilization, primitive cultural leads, and entirely new ideas that emerge and seem consonant with our own times." Tradition innovation could involve major universal events in the life cycle, such as birth, marriage, parenthood, death, puberty rites, religion and worship, birthday and festive occasions, or commemoration of natural events.

[1] Shapiro, S. B. "Explorations in Positive Experience," *LASCP News, 16,* 1964, 11–21.
[2] Shapiro, S. B. "Creativity, Positive Experience, and Ego Therapy," *Explorations,* 1967.

We felt they would profit from at least a sample of this kind of experience because many of them were deeply rooted in tradition but were becoming somewhat uncomfortable with the tired, fundamentalist forms these traditions often took. Most of them were conservative executives and churchmen but with positive and progressive ideals. Their current ideology, we felt, was beginning to emphasize more and more of what Allport calls the proactive side of human affairs.[3] But they were deeply conflicted about it.

Our basic format was to have two trainers for each of the six groups of about twelve people each. Some of the co-trainers each had a separate group; some preferred to think of themselves as two co-trainers with twenty-four-person groups. Much of our initial time, however, was spent in the cluster group formation. In one variant of this format there are inner and outer groups and pair members across the groups themselves. One trainer sits inside with his group while the other trainer sits in the outer circle with his group as observers and the groups are periodically switched (inner to outer and outer to inner).

We originally assigned several general (lecture) sessions to some of our trainers and held one-hour general sessions nearly every day in the five-and-one-half day lab. I was to lead the session on positive experience and tradition innovation. Like many sensitivity-training labs, there was time off scheduled and some special interest groups arranged—for example, one on prayer, and another on values in religious education.

Unlike other groups, however, each day was begun with a worship service conducted by the lab chaplain. The chaplain was a member of the training staff and a participant in one of the training groups. I felt this was a meaningful link between the frankly spiritual aspects of the experience and the "just-as-spiritual" encounters we had in our groups.[4] This link I believe was an additional facilitating force for tradition innovation in this lab.

[3] Allport, G. W. *Pattern and Growth in Personality.* New York: Holt, 1963.
[4] See Clark, J. V. "Toward a Theory and Practice of Religious Experiencing." In J. F. T. Bugental (Ed.) *Challenges of Humanistic Psychology.* New York: McGraw-Hill, 1967.

As usual, I wanted to give my own group an experience in "nonstructure," and after a minimal introduction via name tags, I sat back and waited to see what would develop. The usual things happened. People were anxious for structure. However, many of them had heard of this strange business before and some of them were quite prepared to handle it in one way or another.

Some sat silent, others tried to force structure on the group, and still others made jokes and small talk to fill the dreaded vacuum. At last they seemed to develop a common subject. One man was critical of his organization because it was steeped in tradition of orthodox Sunday school and not receptive to the newer ideas in Christian education. Just as he warmed up to his controversial subject and at about the time he began to be a definite controversial figure in his own right, the cluster time was up, and I interrupted them for pairing. Some of the group were upset at this and questioned the wisdom of the format. I encouraged them to express their feelings in the next group session.

After the short pairing time (ten minutes), my co-trainer's group began much in the same way as mine, but having had the advantage of observing us they were able to fill in the empty spaces with their feelings and observations of us. I sensed that they were a "live" group, and the more outspoken few who took the lead initially favored the expression of feelings—personal feelings in the here-and-now—and even negative feelings they had about one another. These people supported our training goals, and both my co-trainer and I were pleased by this.

However, a strong counterfaction developed. Several of the more assertive people challenged the wisdom of personal expressions of anger, resentment, and even anxiety or discomfort. Most of the opposition in both groups was in the form of sermonettes, the responses to which were more sermonettes advocating the opposite philosophy. My co-trainer and I frequently pointed out the sermonizing but much of it continued until the very end. These people, I decided, just love to talk this way.

At this point I wish to point up the Wednesday morning session leading to tradition innovation. Things seemed to be coming along about right. Everyone on the staff felt the lab was progressing as it should. One could feel the program building nicely. The groups had difficulty with hostile feelings and open confrontations with one another, but they were receptive to the goals of the program, which were more explicitly spelled out in the general sessions—the emphasis on feelings, the idea of personal learning, the laboratory concept, a place where you could test your impact on others and their effect on you, a place to try new behaviors and new role prescriptions, relatively free of the usual structure and pressures.

Wednesday morning, all seventy-five of us, including staff, met in a large room which reminded me of a gymnasium. I stated the underlying positive theme of the morning, emphasizing the need for adults like us, in responsible positions, to learn to play all over again. This need is vital, I stated, not only because we need it as a physical, emotional, and spiritual renewal, but also because it often provided a productive and creative base for our work. Here I used the concepts of inner parent, adult, and child,[5] and I stressed how important I felt it was to learn to let the inner child out in a constructive setting. I said that if creative potential could be released, less energy would be needed for suppression and repression and that the total person would be enriched by redirecting this energy. My theory held that there was a largely unused reservoir of positive feelings in all of us. This reservoir could be tapped to allow the good feelings to "flow upward" and "nourish the ego" for the rest of the week and hopefully for much longer than that.

I related all this to putting zest back into learning, to becoming a person, and to learning this through various artistic and sensory modalities (verbal, nonverbal, body movement, fantasy, children's games, and so on). I stressed again the exploration and extension of positive feelings—learning to go where such feelings took you.

I explained that in order to demonstrate these ideas I would like to divide the group of seventy-five randomly into small groups of six or seven each. The trainers were to fully participate but in their own training group. The morning activity was to consist largely of a series of short exercises each of about ten minutes and each bounded by a five-minute feedback or theory session.

[5] Berne, E. *Games People Play*. New York: Grove Press, 1964.

First I asked them to have a T-group, by which I meant an unstructured interpersonal encounter, much like the groups they were already in. However, the one ground rule in this T-group was that they were to express only positive feelings about themselves or one another. The room began buzzing as they took to the idea. Our trainer group found it easier to express good feelings about one another than about ourselves, but we made a start, and the positive interaction began to grow.

At the end of ten minutes of the positive T-group, I asked for feedback from the various groups, and they said that it was a welcome relief from their original groups, but that they had particular difficulty in praising themselves openly. Some even had trouble expressing positive feelings toward others.

Our next exercise consisted of a repeat of the first T-group, only this time we were to express positive feelings we were reluctant to say in the first exercise. This released considerably more feeling than the first grouping, and in our group several of us were in tears. This was so not only because of our needs to hear the love, affection, and appreciation we had for one another, but also to release some of our own deeper positive, loving feelings about ourselves. In my opinion it was a deeply moving, religious experience for us and for many of the other people in that room. Feedback again was solicited, and it was very favorable—again some shyness, inhibition, and awkwardness was reported; but most of the groups felt very close and warm toward one another. The entire group became a kind of I-Thou love society.

The next exercise was thumb-wrestling, which I demonstrated with one of my fellow trainers. I also demonstrated two-handed thumb-wrestling and group thumb-wrestling. It was a pleasure to see how these outwardly staid, conservative, middle-aged church executives enjoyed this exercise. They acted like a group of children, howling, laughing, moving, and entering into the task with abandon. Most of them enjoyed the physical contact and the combative play. Their competitive needs showed clearly and joyously. The feedback on this was also excellent. They said they enjoyed it, that it loosened them up, and that it was surprising how much they wanted to win—men and women alike.

Switching now to two fantasy exercises, I asked for four

volunteers for the next activity. After a very brief moment of hesitation, four came toward me. These people, I felt, place a very high conscious value on cooperation—and they behaved that way. When the four volunteers reached me in the center of the room, I explained the game. I really did not need the volunteers, so I thanked them and asked them to go back to their group. It was to be a fantasy exercise in which everyone was to have a dialogue between two inner voices—the voice that said "Go ahead and volunteer," and the voice that said "Don't volunteer." I asked them to try to assign a face and person to each of these voices. Again they responded quite readily and they had ten-minute T-groups to share their inner dialogue fantasies. The report back from the groups revealed that some people had difficulty in connecting a face or person with these two inner voices but that most of them were able to have the inner debate. Also they reported that this inner debate had a lot of meaning for them—it represented duty versus desire, or showing off versus withdrawing from the center of attention.

The second fantasy exercise involved imagining the present small group sitting in an open field, and one member of the group getting up. This was to be the starting point for a fantasy which could then move in any direction. It did not matter whether they thought of themselves or one of the others as the one standing. The idea was to take it from there, and then to share the fantasy with the group. Here again a few minutes of silence was introduced to develop the fantasy. The feedback this time was also revealing and mostly favorable. Through this exercise, they stated, they were able to sense some feelings they had about their small group. Certain fears and apprehensions were aired; it also became plain how much the small groups had come to mean to them in this short space of time. It brought out much mutual concern, warmth, and attachment.

After the break I introduced the concept of space-carving. The first kind of space-carving involved each group standing in a circle and each person locating himself in his own surrounding three-dimensional space. To do this they could touch the perimeters of their space with their hands, feet, body, or head. They could crawl through the space or jump up to explore it, and so on. Because of real space limitations several groups moved into an adjoining lounge and several corridors. I interrupted this activity after about five minutes, and asked them to repeat the experience. Most of them seemed somewhat stiff and awkward at first, but gradually they warmed up to the exercise. The small group support they had been building was of great help to the more inhibited ones. They encouraged and supported one another in this "strange" activity. One of my colleagues remarked to me how much it looked like the back ward of a state hospital. I agreed, and felt that this observation was highly significant in that this activity was, in a sense, a regressive activity, far more primitive and basic than the usual verbal stuff in which these people spent most of their time. I saw it as regression in the service of growth.

Our trainer group demonstrated the second kind of space-carving by moving, one at a time, through a rectangular floor space we had set aside in the gymnasium-like room. After moving through this space in pairs, in triads, and finally in the whole group together, we helped the groups set up their own space and move through it in the one, two, three, total group sequence I had suggested. Again they could carve their space in any way they wanted —running, walking, crawling, tumbling, jumping—and at any pace or pattern that suited them. Most of them took to the exercise and were fully involved after their previous warm-ups—and there was much obvious pleasure in this activity. Again I was very impressed with their willingness to participate in what I am sure many people would regard as foolishness.

Having had this sequence of activities to build on, I introduced the idea of tradition innovation. I said that each group would be assigned a task, and that they would be given about twenty minutes to develop their ideas, and then each group would present its results to the total group. I explained to them that I was for tradition, ritual, and ceremony, but that I felt many of our traditions were "tired," and that they could stand some renovating. I suggested that each group come up with a new tradition, ritual, or ceremony to celebrate some event, occasion, or feeling. The medium for this could be nonverbal pantomime, it could be a prayer, or a poem, a story, an idea for a celebration, or the like. The form and content of the new tradition was up to them.

Our trainer group immediately set about to develop a new

tradition, and we first hit on the idea of some brief nonverbal way of expressing the main dimensions of human interaction in a group greeting. It was to be a way of saying hello in such a fashion that we ran through all the ways we could relate to one another. What we developed was based on Horney's[6] three reactions to basic anxiety: moving toward people, moving against people, and moving away from people. We evolved a sequence, beginning with moving toward one another from various distant points in the room, in which we formed a circle facing inward. Our nonverbal greeting ritual consisted of holding hands, moving together as close as we could in the center and holding hands up together, moving back, struggling with each other in an Indian wrestling gesture, then turning our backs on one another. This sequence was repeated and the final gesture was to stand facing one another as we had when we first started the sequence. We demonstrated our ritual when it was our turn.

Each group took about five or ten minutes to demonstrate their new tradition. The following is a description of what evolved.

The first group sang a kind of nursery rhyme to the tune of "Ach Du Lieber Augustine." The rhyme was about the lab, with all of their mixed feelings of apprehension and warmth coming through in the verses. This tradition also involved a child's game of coming in and writing part of the song on the blackboard and changing key words to make them funnier.

A second group proposed a National Relaxation Day. For this day each family was to build, borrow, or steal a kind of large pedestal or platform on which they would put their most significant and representative work tools—for example, saw, hammer, lawn-mower, school books, pots and pans, account books, desk. One of the rules for the day was to eliminate all transportation, public and private, except for health or other emergencies. People were to walk wherever they were going, and families were to visit one another. On the radio and TV there were to be only light, relaxing musical or artistic programs, no speeches, news reports, or any "heavy, serious" programs. National Relaxation Day was to take place on a

---

[6] Horney, K. *Neurosis and Human Growth.* New York: Norton, 1950.

day other than Sunday. There were religious services of a very informal kind for everyone who wanted to attend—but these could
be held in the back yard, with people in play clothes, in a very
relaxed, natural setting. Those who wanted to get out into the
country for walks or picnics were encouraged to do so—but they
had to walk to get there. The ideas were all read in the form of a
national proclamation from the President of the United States. Each
group member read part of the proclamation.

Another ritual was suggested around the event of having a
son or daughter leave the family group before marriage. It was intended to be separate from a marriage ceremony, typically when a
youngster went away to college, or to work, or to the service. The
tradition involved most of a day or several days in which relatives
and friends of the family were invited. Before the friends came
however, the departing one was to spend time with his own family
—perhaps talking about how he felt about leaving, his hopes, plans,
and goals. Feelings were also to be expressed by the parents and
remaining siblings. It was a time for goodbyes—and a preparation
for a new life—a kind of transition ceremony.

One group suggested a graduation ceremony for the end of
the sensitivity-training program. It was to be a peace-pipe kind of
ritual in which the stuff actually smoked was tea leaves in honor of
the T-groups. In this rather corny pun I saw something profound
and significant: sharing the same pipe—which meant in many
Indian tribes a sign of peace between men. It was a kind of common
bond which I think our people felt and expressed by this ritual. I
was also pleased to see a mixing of modern and primitive ceremony,
however superficial it might appear.

There was one group that concentrated on making hello
and goodbye more meaningful. They explained and demonstrated
the Indian, Roman, Christian, and Hebrew greetings and leave-
takings. Another group performed the ancient Japanese tea ceremony, without the pun this time. Also, analogous to the warriors'
having to take off their swords before they entered the teahouse,
they entered their church basement teahouse and checked their
symbolic weapons at the door (hostility, greed, jealousy, arrogance,
fear, and so on). Another ceremony they performed in the new tea-

house was gathering all the old rituals in one pile and burning them. What they actually burned were pieces of paper, representing the old worn-out rituals, and symbolizing their dedication to tradition innovation.

A very impressive ceremony demonstrated by another group involved the eucharist ceremony, the Lord's Supper. This group's idea was to change the Lord's Supper by defrocking the priests and dividing the food among all the people. I did not understand this very well, not being a Christian, but the audience seemed very impressed with its significance.

There were several other groups who had devised new ways of saying hello and goodbye, by special handshakes, by sign language and with special greeting gestures. They were essentially variations on our trainer group's ceremony described above.

One of the most meaningful demonstrations was a pantomime by one group. The only words they used were, "This is the church," pointing to a small circular rug which they had taken from the adjoining lounge. The rug was barely large enough for all six people in the group to sit on it, and they began a rather animated nonverbal communication which represented first the business and then the worship services of the church. Soon one member was singled out and pointed at because he did not conform to the group ritual. Fingers were shaken in his face, and he was driven out of the church, onto the bare floor of the large room. He sat there alone for a time, while the in-group church members went back to their rug church. Shortly after they resumed their transactions it became apparent that they were suffering considerable guilt. They quickly agreed to send someone out into the world and to bring the maverick back to the fold. First a man was delegated, but he was rebuffed by the outcast, and then a woman was sent out. She too was rejected as she pointed the way for the exile to return. After she got back, the church group held a meeting—and they decided to move the whole church "out into the world." They did this by picking up the rug and carrying it to the man outside. Then they invited him in again—and this time he accepted. It was very well done, and most impressive to the people watching.

Perhaps the highlight in the tradition-innovation exercise was one group's presentation of what they called "The Washington

Doctrine of Original Goodness." This was a litany in direct opposition to the doctrines of original sin, and everyone, I think, caught onto this almost immediately. Their litany is quoted below.

The Washington Doctrine of Original Goodness

LEADER: In the beginning God. God is Good. He created Man.

RESPONSE: God looked upon His creation and saw that it was Good.

LEADER: He created Woman.

RESPONSE: God looked upon His creation and saw that it was Good.

LEADER: In love, God, Man, and Woman created a Baby.

RESPONSE: God looked upon His creation and saw that it was Good.

LEADER: Originally, all men are Good.

RESPONSE: God looked upon His creation and saw that it was Good.

LEADER: It is what men do to each other that brings pain and sin into the world.

RESPONSE: God looked upon His creation and saw that it was Good.

LEADER: As man understands his emotions, he becomes closer to his original creation.

RESPONSE: God looked upon His creation and saw that it was Good.

LEADER: Joyful, Joyful, We adore Thee [*This is a hymn sung by leader and congregation*].

RESPONSE: God looked upon His creation and saw that it was Good.

LEADER: and

CONGREGATION: Truly the Lord is Good. Amen.

Reflecting on the tradition-innovation experience, I once more felt that the timing was right and that the background build-up of openness and group spirit was a necessary part of its success. I doubted, and my trainer-colleagues agreed, that this would have been received as well the first or second day. We felt that it came at a most appropriate point in the lab, when many of the groups were tired from struggling with the strange new codes of sensitivity training. We had that afternoon off, and I think most of the participants left with a relaxed, good feeling about themselves and what was happening.

The balance of the lab went well. The groups kept moving and many individuals learned a great deal. People kept remarking about the Wednesday morning activity. Many of them experienced it as one of the highlights of their week—and many assimilated it as a kind of reference experience.

Tradition innovation, it seems to me, helps to integrate the past with the present. It teaches us to value the past, but not to worship it. It shows us that we can enrich the present with past or primitive tradition—to make our present lives more meaningful. It is also a continuity builder, an enterprise which allows us to experience the continuity from our ancestors through our parents to us and through us to our children. Also, I feel tradition innovation is a learning experience. It enables us to share resources about culture. Rituals, ceremonies, and traditions have a common root in the significant events of human life—in all cultures. Thus it tends to unite us and to make us even more aware that our similarities outweigh our differences.

Finally, tradition innovation upends our culture-bound ways of thinking. I believe it refreshes our inventory of current ceremonies, so that instead of becoming ever more antispiritual, antireligious, and antidepth, we can express our universal humanity through revitalized new traditions. These new traditions, I think, are among the many changes we need to make and are beginning to make to reduce the alienation and separation so characteristic of our times. Traditions and spirituality, I believe, are necessary mortar in the structure of our Western society, because they bring us closer to the core of ourselves and our fellow man, living together as we do in profound interdependence. In Eric Havelock's[7] terms, we will have to retribalize ourselves. Perhaps like the pre-platonic ancient Greeks we will have to reestablish tribal encyclopediae. Tradition innovation, as I see it, is one way of helping us to do this.

It may be well to pause at this point and speculate on why this approach was effective. The first point I wish to mention concerns the concept of regression of the service of the ego. Writers like Kris[8] and Menninger[9] have stressed the idea that in psycho-

[7] Havelock, E. A. *Preface to Plato*. Cambridge: Harvard University Press, 1963.

[8] Kris, E. *Psychoanalytic Explorations in Art*. New York: International Universities Press, 1952.

[9] Menninger, K. *Theory of Psychoanalytic Technique*. New York: Basic Books, 1958.

analysis the patient's ego not only must allow the various primary-process productions of the id to erupt into consciousness, but that the ego organization itself must temporarily regress in order for first abreaction and then synthesis to take place. This would be particu-largly true in activities like play and artistic work. Writers on cre-ativity (Barron,[10] Brown,[11] and Moustakas[12]) have stressed the processes and the kinds of people who are perceived as creative. Creative people both in and out of the arts have the capacity not only to allow but to encourage regression to more primitive ways of handling material and thoughts and to emerge with productions generally regarded as artistic, socially useful, or both. Activities like brainstorming[13] are based on the ability to suspend initial evaluation temporarily until after the imagination has been given free reign for associative connections around the problem in question.

Likewise, in tradition innovation the atmosphere is one of experiment and play which releases the potentially creative com-binatorial modes in people. In this particular laboratory this was effective because it occurred after considerable trust building and at a point where small T-group loyalties and warmth had general-ized somewhat to the lab as a whole. The exercise further deepened and extended these trust bonds besause it was set up to provide new small group contacts—with people who were not in the original T-group together. The theory here follows Gibb's idea[14] that goal formation and social control come after the establishment of trust and data flow. It was the opinion of the staff that the same kind of effect could not have taken place the first few days of the lab.

There was another factor operating on the positive side in

[10] Barron, F. "Diffusion, Integration and Enduring Attention in the Creative Process." In R. W. White (Ed.) *The Study of Lives*. New York: Atherton Press, 1963.

[11] Brown, G. I., "An Experiment in the Teaching of Creativity," *The School Review, 72*, 1964.

[12] Moustakas, C. *Creativity and Conformity*. Princeton, N. J.: Van Nostrand, 1967.

[13] Shaw, M. E. "Group Dynamics." In P. R. Farnsworth (Ed.) *Annual Review of Psychology*. Palo Alto: Annual Reviews, 1961.

[14] Gibb, J. R. "Climate for Trust Formation." In L. P. Bradford, J. R. Gibb, and K. D. Benne (Eds.), *T-Group Theory and Laboratory Method*. New York: Wiley, 1964.

this particular laboratory: the church executives were already closely identified with certain symbols, rituals, and ceremonies. Not only were many of them formerly ministers who are by definition purveyors and interpreters of ceremony, ritual, and tradition, but they were almost to a man deeply religious people. This receptivity to symbolism and especially spiritual symbolism ties closely with the major basic professed value system of Christianity—brotherly love and worship of God. Their traditional ingrained desire for harmony and unity as Christians was also buttressed by the kind of Christians they were. As members of the "liberal" National Council of Churches they were identified with change—at least ideologically. The whole policy of the Church Executive Development Board included receptivity to change and so used sensitivity-training groups or encounter groups to facilitate personal growth—and help adapt these people and the church to change in the world. Phrases like "the living church" and "the church-in-the-world" were very popular with these people. So, they were not only oriented to tradition— but also to innovation.

Another powerful factor in promoting the impact of this exercise was the warm feelings most of the participants had toward the staff and vice versa. The general atmosphere of the lab was trusting and warm. The fact that the staff of trainers first demonstrated some of the exercises as a small group not only served as a model for the participants but also provided considerable self-disclosure. The self-disclosures of the staff came in the form of playful nonverbal and verbal exercises and in the presentations of tradition innovation itself. Jourard,[15] Culbert,[16] Clark,[17] and others[18] have found that self-disclosure often has a salutary effect on groups and

[15] Jourard, S. *The Transparent Self*. Princeton, N. J.: Van Nostrand, 1964.

[16] Culbert, S. "Trainer Self-Disclosure and Member Growth in Two T-Groups." *Journal of Applied Behavioral Science, 4,* 1968, 47–73.

[17] Clark, J. V., and Culbert, S. A. "Mutually Therapeutic Perception and Self-Awareness in a T-Group." *Journal of Applied Behavioral Science, 1,* 1965, 180–194.

[18] Whitaker, C. A., and Warkentin, J. "The Therapist as Prototype." In J. F. T. Bugental (Ed.) *Challenges of Humanistic Psychology.* New York: McGraw-Hill, 1967.

individuals like this. From another theoretical perspective the staff leadership was accepted as defining, presenting, and maintaining a certain definition of the situation. There was a working consensus on this definition of the situation. This follows the sociological thinking of Thomas,[19] Goffman,[20] and Volkart.[21]

The question now arises whether the learning experiences and principles from this lab apply to other encounter groups or human relations labs. Answering this question requires abstracting and generalizing these principles. Thus, we can observe the following conditions: (1) regression in the service of the individual and collective ego was encouraged and supported; (2) this occurred in the middle of the laboratory experience after trust bonds and warmth had been established; (3) the participants were already oriented ideologically toward both tradition and innovation; (4) the whole experience was supported by the staff's participation, which reinforced and supported the experience by the principles of modeling and self-disclosure.

Perhaps we can see that favorable conditions existed for the tradition-innovation experience and that similar favorable general conditions would likely facilitate favorable outcomes in other settings. Factors like the encouragement of play, body movement, self-disclosure, and trust acted to reinforce one another to produce the observed effect. Thus, if norms of expressive participation are carefully built and encouraged by a trusted staff and the activity in question is properly timed and the participants are already committed to a similar ideology, the definition of the learning situation is likely to reach a stable consensus. Learning is therefore likely to be facilitated. I believe these principles would hold for any group.

Now, I would like to say a word about this approach as compared to classical dyadic or group therapy formats. In my opinion the types of encounter group or human relations labs like

[19] Thomas, W. I. "Situational Analysis: The Behavior Pattern and the Situation." In M. Janowitz (Ed.) *On Social Organization and Social Personality*. Chicago: University of Chicago Press, 1966.

[20] Goffman, E. *The Presentation of Self in Everyday Life*. New York: Doubleday, 1959.

[21] Volkart, E. H. (Ed.) *Social Behavior and Personality*. New York: Social Science Research Council, 1951.

the one presented in this chapter do not replace individual psychotherapy but greatly expand its possibilities. This is true because the
client or patient is exposed to many more stimuli in the here-and-
now in greatly expanded response modalities of artistic, verbal, and
nonverbal types. In other words, there is much more to respond to
and many more alternatives of response to be observed and experienced by the self and others in the here-and-now. The here-and-
now potential for psychological growth is stressed by most human-
istically oriented psychologists like Maslow,[22] Perls,[23] Rogers,[24] and
others. With people as characterologically restrained as many of the
church executives are likely to be, this greater freedom of both
stimulus and response is considered an advantage in line with the
desired outcomes stated earlier in the chapter. With constricted
adults—as many of us are these days—techniques which loosen and
open people are preferable to more limited, classical, verbal approaches like psychoanalysis or even classical nondirective therapy.

Feedback which I have personally received from many
patients and therapists who have had much exposure to both traditional group therapy and encounter groups indicate that the latter
are much more exciting and meaningful but need to be reinforced
by the ongoing weekly therapy session of the more traditional sort.
Some of the most important effects of weekend marathon groups,
for example, seem to fade over time unless periodically and preferably regularly enforced. A kind of synthesis of traditional group
therapy and encounter group methods has been occurring in the
practices of many psychologists and psychiatrists—apparently with
the advantages of both approaches and without some of the disadvantages.

[22] Maslow, A. H. *Toward a Psychology of Being*. Princeton, N. J.:
Van Nostrand, 1962.

[23] Perls, F., Hefferline, R., and Goodman, P. *Gestalt Therapy*. New
York: Dell, 1951.

[24] Rogers, C. R. "The Process of the Basic Encounter Group." In
J. F. T. Bugental (Ed.) *Challenges of Humanistic Psychology*. New York:
McGraw-Hill, 1967.

XIII

Encounter in Higher Education

Sumner B. Morris
Jack C. Pflugrath
Barbara Taylor

Henry Seidel Canby, former student and professor at Yale University, wrote of college life in America in the 1890's and at the turn of the century citing the gap between faculty and students and how the two groups functioned at cross-purposes. He portrayed the faculty member with his emphasis on scholarship and pedantic specialization and his frequently futile efforts to reach the "future political, social, commercial, and industrial leadership of the United States. . . ." and said that "the faculty of those days . . . had one of the great opportunities of educational history, and muffed it."

Many faculty were "scholars bred in the idea that their sacred knowledge was a temple set apart from everyday life." Writing as a former student, he said: "We were supposed to forget our concern with living while we studied their theories; but this was not made easier by their concern to separate what they knew from any close references to contemporary life . . . they had lost the power of relating what they knew to what we knew, and hence, even when fertile in research, were sterile as leaders—or guides."[1]

Today, more than half a century later, few would maintain that the higher education experience has remained entirely as Canby described it in those days. Due largely to an affluent and democratic America, which forced open the doors of higher learning to a more diversified, more egalitarian student body, higher education has flourished. Yet contemporary students and critics of higher education raise a familiar cry. The question of relevant, personally meaningful educational experience is still insistently present. College administrators, from the huge, state systems of the West Coast, to the ivy league campuses of the East, are daily confronted by an increasing number of activist students who no longer seem content to accept the traditional education pattern as adequate to their needs and potentialities. While the motivations and purposes of those demanding change vary, the fact remains that there is considerable dissent among a restless and discontented generation of students. A common thread appears in much of what they demand; they want an educational experience relevant to their needs and the complexities of the contemporary world and more active participation in their own education.

For those who have worked intimately with students and know them as persons, the existential questioning and often vociferous demands come as no surprise. College students, especially at the more select, intellectually demanding schools, have changed markedly during the past few years. Keniston[2] describes them as "an unusually serious, well-informed, honest and morally concerned group. While they scorn the round of fun and frivolity that dominated the

---

[1] Canby, H. S. *Alma Mater*. New York: Farrar, 1936.

[2] Keniston, K. "Heads and Seekers: Drugs on Campus, Counter Cultures, and American Society," *American Scholar, 38,* 1968, 97–112.

lives of previous college generations, they in fact care deeply about one another, and a growing number are intensely concerned with the social and political future of their world."

Questions which would have brought an embarrassed silence from their apathetic peers of the fifties, or perhaps would have been dismissed as abstruse "intellectualism," are now openly acknowledged by many college students with thoughtfulness and intensity. What really matters to an increasing number of college students is not academic performance with the subsequent rewards of acquisition and status, but concerns of a quite different nature. The differences between students today and students of the fifties can partly be understood by the questions they ask: What is significant? What is the good life? What is morality? How can I love? What is worthwhile? What matters and what do I stand for? How can I make connections with my own feelings and the feelings of others?

What are some of the changes students ask for? Mainly, they ask for more direct and personal involvement in class work, more relatedness between what happens in class and life experience, and a deeper, personal, more meaningful relationship with the more knowing member of the class experience, the professor. One of the most important words to students is *personal*. In relating the most significant and satisfying experience during their four years in college, students invariably look to the time a professor took a personal interest in them or a project in which they felt involved and needed.

Despite the official litany that higher education should aim at the total development of the student, such is seldom the case. Much of what actually happens continues to be dominated by the traditional ethos of passive and heady cognitive training with the rewards going almost exclusively to students who read the system well and then conform. Indeed, students are usually forced to spend so much time and energy in purely academic and intellectual pursuits that crucially important life-related concerns have to be put aside or bootlegged as best they can. To a sometimes confused, often pressured college student this bootlegging is often haphazard and seldom sufficient. Thus, while technical skill and fact learning are often achieved, many students will have graduated with their

192 Encounter in Higher Education

quest for personal knowledge, relatedness, and sense of identity largely unfulfilled. And for many of them, unless they are quite fortunate, a second chance will not be forthcoming.

Persons who have sought to know students in depth come to strikingly similar conclusions about needed innovation and change.[3] Most emphasize the importance of an integration of the affective domain—feelings and emotions, sensitivity, personal awareness, interpersonal relationships, creativity, imagination—with the cognitive domain—"knowing things," cognitive styles, and the accumulation of facts. Learning and experience in the affective domain are now often left to chance and sometimes even viewed as subversive to the "real" purposes and goals of higher education. That this should be the case is rather remarkable in view of the abundance of psychological evidence that shows the pervasive effect of emotions on cognitive learning. As Brown says, "The individual potential of each student is nowhere near realized because of the lack of attention to the student's emotional life—to the powerful motivators and sustainers such as anxiety, fear, hunger, insecurity, sex, joy, love, hate and loneliness, and the human needs for identity, connectedness, and a sense of personal power which grow out of these emotions." Significant and relevant learning rarely occurs, if at all, without the support of the affective domain. Innovation in higher education is urgently needed to offset the often impersonal, dehumanizing academic experience, and to help students find their identity, their "selves," and their "wholeness." There seems to be occurring a confluence of T-group or sensitivity-training techniques and Gestalt theory and technique from which the encounter group is springing. This small group approach, bringing persons together in an atmosphere of community and trust, fairly explodes with antidotes for what ails higher education. Students want a relevant education: the basic mode of the encounter group is relevance, the actual, the

[3] Brown, G. I. "A Project for Planning the Organization and Operation of Two Regional Program Centers for Humanistic Education." Proposal to Ford Foundation, 1968; Farson, R. "Emotional Barriers to Education," *Psychology Today, 1,* 1967, 33–35; Katz, J., and others. *No Time for Youth.* San Francisco: Jossey-Bass, 1968; Maslow, A. H. *Religions, Values, and Peak Experiences.* Columbus: Ohio State University, 1964; Sanford, N. *Where Colleges Fail.* San Francisco: Jossey-Bass, 1967.

real, and the here-and-now. For an environment which strives to be a community of scholars, the encounter process stresses openness, transparency, and clear and effective communication. Its basic premium is the potential of persons to facilitate the growth and development of persons. It helps reduce the barriers of roles and styles of living which keep apart and prevent understanding.

Encounter group techniques can be used in several ways in higher education. In addition to their appearance in student service programs, such as counseling centers, psychological clinics, and deans of students programs, they have application to the classroom. One such classroom experiment was conducted at the University of California, Davis, in a psychology class titled "Personal and Social Adjustment."

This course in personal and social adjustment encompasses a kind of "understanding-yourself-and-others" psychology. It has traditionally been taught in the usual academic manner with the instructor giving lectures and the students taking notes and feeding back the information at examination time. The course, which is primarily taken as an elective by students, seemed especially well-suited for the implementation of some type of small group laboratory in interpersonal relations. Thus, in this experiment, the lectures were reduced in number and an encounter group format was introduced as part of the course experience. Each student received at least eighteen hours of interpersonal lab or encounter group experience for the academic quarter in groups that averaged ten in size. Psychologists from the counseling center at UCD served as leaders in the groups. The experience was structured as follows in an outline distributed to students at the beginning of the class:

> The main focus of Psychology 33 will be small group experience. You will meet with a group of 8 to 10 fellow students once a week for approximately two hours (the time may vary somewhat between groups) in a kind of interpersonal laboratory in which personal encounter and sensitivity to self and others will be emphasized. This experience will provide an opportunity to bring down the conceptual and abstract (the content of the course) to a more personally relevant and meaningful level. The purpose is to stimulate self-examination and awareness through the experience of listening and being listened to and receiving

feedback about "how you come across to others." The emphasis
is on growth and development.

To assess student reaction to the course, questionnaires were
completed by the students at the end of each of the two academic
quarters in which encounter group methods were utilized. At the
end of the first quarter, the students found that the addition of the
encounter groups increased their involvement in the course and
made it a much more meaningful and relevant experience when
compared with other college courses already taken. During the
second quarter, encounter groups were used exclusively in one section of the class (without lectures) and compared to a lecture
group control (without encounter groups) in another section.
Students in the encounter group section not only found their experience more personally meaningful and relevant when compared
with the traditional lecture section but also performed as well as
the lecture section on the assigned content of the course.

Perhaps the most dramatic data of this study come from the
phenomenological descriptions of their experience by the students
themselves:

> One of the most valuable experiences I've gotten from a
> course was the encounter groups. It was one of the few times
> I've felt a course related to actual life. I would like to do it
> again because I think it helped my view of myself and others.

> These were fantastic learning experiences for me. I think
> they definitely help one to see himself more clearly. They are a
> comfort in anxiety.

> One of the most worthwhile innovations in higher educa-
> tion since who-knows-when. Requires and stimulates true involve-
> ment of the student.

> I was glad to be able to talk about things I don't usually
> get a chance to discuss. I became more aware of myself and
> more able to accept some ideas about me.

> The encounter groups really "made" the class. I gained a
> lot of personal insight and am learning even more. Don't *ever*
> knock these groups out. It helped so much—academically *and*
> personally!

> The encounter group was the real basis of the course—

it enabled me to see what the reading actually meant and to see my problems and strengths in relation to others.

This is the first time I have ever really become involved with a class. I feel like I can really express "me" without any fear of social disapproval as I feel in other situations.

A unique experience that I will never forget.

Fantastic experience!

This class has been the best thing that ever happened to me: besides being born (for now I realize my life is important).

We are particularly pleased with these tentative outcomes because we believe they reflect an excitement and involvement not usually found in established college courses. We believe that the important value of the course was the *integration* between the affective-experiential domain and the conceptual-cognitive domain. We conceived our task as one of providing the students with conceptual learnings and then of integrating these learnings in a more effective and relevant manner by providing concrete, experiential correlates in an encounter group setting. The meshing of cognitive information with affective experience was clearly illustrated by one class member who felt impelled to read aloud three pages of text on the concepts of self. This was warmly received by her responsive audience who had, the week before, participated in the quite dramatic emergence of "the real me" in a group setting. Morris, Pflugrath, and Emery[4] present a more detailed account of the method and results of this study.

The implications of bringing encounter group methodology to other courses of the curriculum, especially those with heavy emphasis on content and intellectual rigor, are exciting and challenging. We believe, for example, that many of the traditional classroom procedures seem designed almost to preclude effective learning.

Close inspection of the actual classroom situation often reveals a scene that has an element of absurdity. Asking the typical intelligent, self-activating young adult to sit passively for fifty minutes of lecturing with little opportunity to express his questions, feelings,

[4] Morris, S., and Pflugrath, J. "Personal Encounter in Higher Education," *Personnel and Guidance Journal* (in press).

ideas, insights, and even his boredom denigrates whatever there is of human potential. Turned around and viewed from the instructor's perspective, it is equally inefficient. It is possible for a large majority of a lecture class to be completely confused or bored, and there are few open channels for the instructor to receive the feedback that tells him how he comes across. It is true that many schools have instructor evaluations, but usually after the course has ended. What is needed for all parties involved in the classroom operation is some type of immediate working relationship or intraclass communication process that deals with what is happening in an open and direct here-and-now manner.

In a typical four-unit lecture course (an academic quarter term) approximately forty hours of time are spent in the classroom. What would result if one tenth of the time or four hours were spent in group communication-building activity? Such activity would focus on both the instructor and the students knowing each other somewhat better as persons with a consequent transparency about personal goals, anxieties, satisfactions, strengths, weaknesses, and so on. Would the one-tenth time lost to the group-building result in an erosion of the acquisition of knowledge and understanding of the subject matter? It is our opinion that it would not. These premises fairly clamor for testing and researching.

At the University of California at Davis counseling center we have recently incorporated personal growth experiences based on encounter group method as a regular part of the counseling center services to students. We have increasingly come to view our role as providing affective domain learning and experience to all students who seek it. This sets us somewhat apart from the traditional counseling center purview of assisting students to cope with the classroom and prepare for the job market. We view our function not so much as providing help for the "disturbed" or vocationally oriented student (although we do that too) as for providing affective domain experience for the "normal" college student seeking paths to productive, satisfying, and creative living.

Our conceptual framework for personal growth groups with college students draws heavily from the Gestalt theory and technique as set forth by Perls,[5] the traditional T-group approach of the National Training Laboratory at Bethel, Maine, and the more recent innovations developed by Schutz[6] and others at Esalen Institute. The basic premise of our approach is that students will grow in self-actualizing directions to the extent of their willingness to let down defensive barriers, get in touch with their feelings, and permit a conscious awareness of feeling to emerge in the ongoing present, the here and now. The idea is that growth can only occur in the present conscious continuum of awareness in which the actual, the real, can be experienced, acknowledged, and "owned." The group leader, or facilitator, aids the process of growth of individuals and of the group by helping the group stay on a here-and-now feeling level, by making explicit what is implicit or unacknowledged in words, feelings, or gestures, and by pointing to the obvious (the belief that people are often unaware of the obvious, of how they relate to others, has been consistently confirmed in our groups). The group leader encourages and fosters the ground rule of the group, which is openness, directness, and honesty between group members. Excessive verbiage, intellectualizing, and analysis are discouraged by the group leader as discursive and viewed as ways persons habitually use to stay outside themselves and away from their true feelings. It is made explicit and clear in our groups that the responsibility for growth and change rests exclusively with the individual. A basic premise is that when the leader or others in the group "feels a feeling" or "explains away a feeling" for the experiencing person, he is denying that person, at that moment, a chance for growth.

Both verbal and nonverbal techniques are used in our groups. We have found several nonverbal techniques to be excellent ways of upending the expectations that college students often carry with them to a college- or university-sponsored formal learning experience. These techniques usually communicate much more powerfully than words what we mean by trust, openness, connecting with feel-

---

[5] Perls, F. *Ego, Hunger, and Aggression: A Revision of Freud's Theory and Method.* Big Sur, Calif.: Orbit-Esalen, 1966.
[6] Schutz, W. *Joy.* New York: Grove Press, 1967.

ings, and relating to others. Some of the techniques involve communicating by touch and by eye contact. For example, groups are sometimes begun by asking students to hold hands in two parallel lines and then to simply hold eye contact with the person opposite them for about thirty seconds before moving to the next person and repeating the same exercise. The idea here is to enable the participants to see each other with the usual verbal exchanges and cues eliminated—with an additional emphasis on seeing and observing while being in a physical community (holding hands) with others.

Another technique is the blind walk. In the blind walk, one student, who is blindfolded, leads another through the immediate physical environment and tries to expose him to a variety of sensory experiences. This involves trusting the partner and using senses other than sight—touch, smell, and hearing—to experience and know the environment. In being led, students respond to cues such as pressure on the wrist or a hand on the waist. They touch lampshades, light switches, furniture, grass, leaves, buildings, and each other. What they experience depends primarily upon the imagination and creativity of their leader. After building a sense of trust, some leaders are able to descend or ascend stairs with their partners and whirl or run with them. After about twenty minutes, the leader-follower roles are reversed. It is not only experiencing the texture, temperature, and other qualities of objects in a more intense way that seems important to persons, but the accelerated communication—the sending and receiving of cues between leaders and followers—that establishes new channels of communication. And in brief, it seems impossible for persons in the groups to touch and communicate in this way and not to know and be known to the others to a greater degree.

We should emphasize that the value of most nonverbal techniques lies not only in the nonverbal experience itself, but also in the subsequent articulation of the feelings evoked by the experience. It is very important to provide group members time to react to the exercise and to verbalize the feelings they have experienced in order for a more full and meaningful integration of the experience to be realized. In his book, *Joy*, Schutz describes and provides rationale for the use of a number of nonverbal exercises.[7]

Some of the verbal exercises we use with college groups seem disarmingly simple yet, when legitimized in the group process, become important catalysts for effective communication and personal growth. The group is occasionally broken into smaller microgroups of three to four persons or dyads of two in order to maximize the opportunity of individual expression and relating how things are. We have found that asking participants to complete a sentence, such as: "I am aware of . . . ," "Right now I feel . . . ," "I become lonely when . . . ," or "I am anxious about . . . ," frequently is all the structure needed for group members to be themselves, communicate that self to the group, and begin interrelating. In the two-person dyads each person takes three to five minutes to find, as best he can, what the other person is like as a human being. Each person then intrduces or presents his partner to the rest of the group.

Another verbal exercise is the in-group–out-group discussion model, which, in the encounter group used in our personal and social adjustment course, seemed especially effective for the application of issues from the students' reading and lectures. Each student chose another student from the group to serve as his "counselor." After pairing off in this manner, one member of each pair was asked to be part of an "in-group," with the other member joining an "out-group." Each counselor in the out-group observed his partner in the in-group, which was given a task to discuss. Dealing with one's aggressive feelings and handling fears were examples of some of the structured tasks. After about fifteen minutes, the discussion of the in-group ended and the pairs of students met privately to discuss the experience. The counselor in the out-group had been told to listen not only to what his partnes says, but the manner in which he says it, and how he functioned in the group. After the interaction of the pairs, the process is reversed with the students in the counselor roles becoming the in-group.

Fantasy is also used as a means of uncovering basic wishes

[7] Schutz, *op. cit.*

and wants, conflicts, and inner attitudes toward oneself. Asking students to "close your eyes and imagine that you are climbing a mountain," frequently reveals significant cues as to what the student is really feeling. After each fantasy, each member of the group is invited to share his experience and discuss it. Heavy interpretations are discouraged. The significant interpretation can only rest with the student and what it means phenomenologically to him.

Whether the person climbs the mountain alone or with other people, who the other people in the fantasy are, the view, how he goes about it, and the location and nature of the mountain often suggest meaningful material for discussion and further self-exploration. In one group, a student reported falling into a crevasse with no one to help him get out—a fantasy which was later confirmed by her stated feelings of isolation and apartness.

The techniques described above represent only a few of the many techniques we have experimented with and found useful with college student groups. We believe they add a new and vital dimension to the analytical group process which has traditionally emphasized the symbolic to the almost total exclusion of the actual, the real, the here-and-now.

In summary, our message here is that higher education need respond to what its knowledgeable critics and its student patrons are saying. Higher education, charged with the liberation of the human potential, is in crisis. It can not return to the good old days of unapproachable, detached professors and passive students, nor can it let itself become submerged in destructive confrontation politics and anarchistic revolution. If it is to retain its dignity and meet its purposes, it must demonstrate its capacity for change and its stature as a self-renewing institution. In a very insightful essay entitled "Only Self-Renewing Institutions Can Handle Today's Revolutions,"[8] John W. Gardner, former Secretary of Health, Education, and Welfare, writes about the decay of human institutions and the need to "undertake imaginative redesign of institutions." He states: "The true task is to design a society (and institutions) capable of continuous change, continuous renewal, continuous re-

---

[8] Gardner, J. W. "Only Self-Renewing Institutions Can Handle Today's Revolutions," *Los Angeles Times,* January 1, 1969.

sponsiveness to human need." In listing the attributes of a society capable of renewing itself, Gardner stresses good internal communication, a high degree of individual participation, means of resolving human conflicts, and an educational system that promotes self-discovery, lifelong learning, and the release of individual potential.

As an institution within our society, how does our system of higher education measure up on the criterion of self-renewal? Perhaps this is an unanswerable question in our time. But the question still remains and Gardner's criteria are powerful instigators for action. We have attempted here to establish a case for the recognition of what students are really like as whole persons and for creating the kind of learning environment that accepts their wholeness— their affective life as well as their cognitive.

While encounter group processes have been our focus, they are not espoused as a panacea, but as an example of the kind of self-learning that is the core of higher learning. Carl Rogers[9] has said that ". . . the most important social invention of this century is the encounter group. The demand is utterly beyond belief." What is there about the human condition that brings such a response and are there not important implications in this human phenomenon for higher learning processes?

INDEX